*Fictive Discourse and the
Structures of Literature*

Fictive Discourse and the Structures of Literature

A Phenomenological Approach

FÉLIX MARTÍNEZ-BONATI

Translated by PHILIP W. SILVER
with the author's collaboration

CORNELL UNIVERSITY PRESS

Ithaca and London

Parts of this book originally appeared in *La estructura de la obra literaria,* ©
Félix Martínez Bonati, 1960, 1972, © Editorial Seix Barral, S.A.-Barcelona,
1972; Depósito Legal Ley 11.723.

First published 1981 by Cornell University Press.
Published in the United Kingdom by Cornell University Press Ltd.,
Ely House, 37 Dover Street, London WiX 4AH.

International Standard Book Number 0-8014-1308-7
Library of Congress Catolog Card Number 80-23628
Printed in the United States of America
*Librarians: Library of Congress cataloging information appears
on the last page of the book.*

Josef König in memoriam

Contents

Contents

Contents

Preface

This English edition contains the main theoretical parts of my book *La estructura de la obra literaria* (Santiago: Ediciones de la Universidad de Chile, 1960; Barcelona: Editorial Seix Barral, 1972). The original text has been faithfully translated by Philip W. Silver, a minor part rewritten by me in English and corrected with his help. I have not included in the present volume the prefaces to the Spanish editions, their introductions, or a few rather marginal chapters that deal mostly with authors not generally known to British and American scholars. On the other hand, this edition contains three new sections (written directly in English and corrected with the translator's assistance): Section 17, on derivative logical structures of narratives; Appendix IV, discussing, in terms elaborated in Chapters II and III, Roman Jakobson's concept of poetic and linguistic functions; and Appendix V, remarks on Barbara Herrnstein Smith's and Richard Ohmann's views on the language of literature.

The general themes of this study are the nature of literary discourse and the fundamental architecture of the literary work.

Preface

By "literary work" I mean the object of the ordinary reader's enjoyment—strictly, the object that is constituted and appears in his or her aesthetic experience. The outstanding precedent for such an inquiry is Roman Ingarden's *Das literarische Kunstwerk* (Halle, 1931; Tübingen, 1965; English translation [*The Literary Work of Art*] by George G. Grabowicz, including an introduction by the translator and a foreword by David Michael Levin, Evanston, Ill., Northwestern University Press, 1973). I devote a chapter to critical remarks on Ingarden's view of literary structure. In a more than thematic respect, my work has its immediate source in Josef König's logical-ontological development of the phenomenology of life.

Within the variety of present trends in literary theory and criticism, there appears to be a renewed interest in the subjects considered here. The problem of the logical properties of fictional sentences (dealt with in Chapter I), the theory of the functions of discourse and the semiotic analysis of communication (outlined in Chapter II), the ontological status of literary discourse and the possibility of a nonhistorical literary system of genres (examined in Chapter III), and the analysis of the act of reading and of literary competence (touched on throughout my book and formulated in the Appendixes) are all subjects that have claimed the attention of many in recent years. In the notes I have included references to the most pertinent publications on these matters.

Jonathan Culler, in his *Structuralist Poetics* (Ithaca, Cornell University Press, 1975), after a survey of the critical advances of the last decades and as a kind of prospectus for the future development of literary theory, proposes a poetics that would be a theory of the tacit conventions which constitute the reader's literary competence, his or her proficiency in correctly reading a poetic text. The literary work, according to Professor Culler, can be experienced only through these traditional and for the most part unconscious determinants of the reception of literature. Twenty years ago in this book I formulated (and in part developed) such a program in Kantian terms as the study of the conditions for the possibility of poetic experience or of its transcendental forms. Despite the elapsed time, readers may find that the constitutive forms dealt with by me are of a more basic order than those considered by Professor Culler and by the French Structuralists Roland Barthes, Gérard Genette, and Tzvetan Todorov. Current critical and theoretical concerns with literary reception and with the generative reconstruction of literary works are various and complex, and a claim to priority—on this point as well as on the ontological and logical characterization of literary discourse, the description of the communication structure of the literary object, and others—is not what I want to present to justify the renewed publication of my work. Although certain of the topics I dealt with have been touched on subsequently by others, the view of the nature and constitution of literature that I offer has not, to my knowledge, been articulated anywhere else. The development of a phenomenological theory of literature has been a discontinuous process, and such a theoretical enterprise is still in its beginnings.[1]

The point of view of progress and novelty which I have just invoked is not without problems, at least so far as the theory of literature is concerned. In the sixteenth century as well as in the twentieth, theory has in part been developed by recourse to Aristotle. The demands of my own inquiry caused me to move from René Wellek and Austin Warren's theory of literature, Wolfgang Kayser's method of interpretation, Ingarden's ontology, and Vosslerian-Spitzerian stylistics to Karl Bühler's, Bertrand Russell's, and Edmund Husserl's studies of language and meaning, Ferdinand de Saussure's structuralism, Benedetto Croce's aesthetics, and on back to Kant's transcendental deduction and Aristotle's theory of apophansis and of poetry. Although this book has certain things in common with the structuralist conceptions which appeared later, the notion of structure and the methodological tools that I have applied are considerably older than contemporary structuralist thought.

Desirable change that is referred to with the metaphor of progress is, of course, not always toward novelty. The mutations of scholarly life are complex; although there is an almost organized growth in some parts of our discipline (in the theory of narrative, for instance), there is a continual loss of previously obtained insights in other parts of it which may be more submissive to abrupt displacements of attention or to the paradigm of periodical intellectual revolutions. Many discarded problems have not been solved or appreciably clarified, but at a given moment simply abandoned. Apparently untouched by these vogues, there persist essential questions that make Aristotle's *Poetics* or Kant's *Critiques* statements of immediate actuality. The impulse to understand better what has been there all along is no less conducive to the benefits of philosophic reflection, it seems to me, than the search for new perspectives.

Essential questions indeed reappear again and again in the history of literary theory, or they stir unrecognized beneath efforts and failures: Are the assertive sentences of literary texts true or false, all true, all false, or neither true nor false? Is there an essential difference between literary discourse (in the narrow sense of "literature" that corresponds to the wide sense of "poetry") and ordinary discourse, nonpoetic literature, journalistic or historical narrative? What is the structure of the phenomenon of speech as a human action? How is this structure reflected in literary speech, how in different literary forms or genres? We find these questions and/or responses to them in the works of Plato and Aristotle, Sir Philip Sidney and Samuel Taylor Coleridge, Gottlob Frege and J. L. Austin, and many more, as well as in the pages of this study.

These themes are not gathered here as a loose assortment of critical topics. My discussions of the various subjects are designed to constitute a single line of thought on the nature of literary discourse and the basic architecture of the objects it brings to imagination. I must emphasize, regarding the unity and order of this book, that because the concepts developed and terminologically fixed in early sections are used in subsequent ones, most of my analyses will be misunderstood if read without knowledge of what precedes them in the text. This conceptual order determined the separation of some chapters that are thematically contiguous but correspond to different stages of the elucidation of the general theme.

I hope that I will not induce confusion by adding now that in the order not of exposition but of things, the first and fundamental property of literature is the one examined in Chapter III. Literary discourse is purely imaginary, that is, fictitious, nonreal discourse. From that basic property or modality of being arise the other major phenomena here described: the purely imaginary and tendentially fantastic nature of the communicative situation of literary speech, and the logical particularities of its propositions, that are not possible in real discourse. I did not discuss this basic phenomenon in the initial sections of the book because logical structure (Chapter I), which is related only to the *referential* aspect of linguistic meaning, is more directly approached in a discussion starting from ordinary language and current terms, and also because the analysis of ordinary (real) discourse (Chapter II) is necessarily prior to that of purely imaginary, literary discourse. This design of the process of conceptual elaboration (of course not the only possible design) makes the order of presentation irreversible unless the text is to be entirely rewritten. The reader who has gone through the book to the end will reorder in his mind the parts of the theory according to the *ordo rerum,* or to different principles of construction, not necessarily moving (after the first time, the actual reading) from the more noticeable features to their foundation—that is, according to the disposition I have chosen.

The essence of literature brought to light by this inquiry is *imagination,* not language, since the language of literature is only one, if in a certain respect the basic one, of its imaginary elements. Once we see literature as a purely imaginary objectivity born or reborn in a reader's act of fantasy, we can understand its notable and deviant features (logical, epistemological, stylistic) as specific possibilities of fantasy, not of reality. The question of the relation of literature (a form of fantasy) to reality can then be reopened upon a broader ground.

I cannot discuss here some recent critical notions that might be marginally pertinent to our subject, such as intertextuality and deconstruction. Suffice it to say that in spite of other considerable differences, these new approaches often perform that same reduction of the literary work to its prerequisite elements for which I criticize Ingarden. The tissue of several codes, the interminable strings of *interpretants,* the uninterrupted continuity of texts—in short, all that some critics now adduce as the course and nature of literary experience—is nowhere to be found in a straightforward reading of literature, but rather before or beneath it. The experience of poetry moves in the opposite direction: it articulates and constructs, creates presences and sets limits, objectifies and highlights, and makes use of codes that we possess, to produce a meaning that is conclusive and universal. The literary experience is each time *final* and *closed.* For this reason it can be only imaginary. It may be that our contemporary civilization, by detaching imaginative arts from the word (and at the same time promoting, through its universities, the multiple retextualization of poetic contents), opens on the one hand new paths to intellectual discovery and, on the other, is detrimental to traditional literary experience. Certain recent critical trends may well be a function of this erosion of the form of spiritual life peculiar to the literature of the imagination, to poetry in the widest sense. For the rest, there is a radical difference between the subject of our study and post-Structuralist trends. Our task has not been the creation of new modalities of reading, but the descriptive explication of the traditional institution of literary experience—of the manner of reading which has predetermined, at least down to the present, the creation of literary works of art.

In other publications I have further developed the ideas introduced here: on the logical themes, see ''Die logische Struktur der Dichtung'' (*Deutsche Vierteljahrsschrift für Literaturwis-*

senschaft und Geistesgeschichte, 1973); on the theory of the functions of speech, "Algunos tópicos estructuralistas y la esencia de la poesía" (*Revista Canadiense de Estudios Hispánicos*, Vol. II, No. 3, 1978); on the concept of imaginary discourse, "The Act of Writing Fiction" (*New Literary History*, Spring 1980); on the analysis of the act of reading and literary competence, "Lectura y crítica" (*Revista Canadiense de Estudios Hispánicos*, Vol. I, No. 2, 1977), and "Erzählungsstruktur und ontologische Schichtenlehre" (*Erzählforschung I*, ed. W. Haubrichs, Göttingen, 1976).

To my colleague Philip Silver I am indebted not only for his proposing and accomplishing this translation, but also for the encouragement he has given to my theoretical work. If the English of the text is sometimes awkward, it is due to my wish to preserve perhaps nonexistent shades of meaning, and to his friendly deference to that wish. From Bernhard Kendler and his (for me) anonymous readers I have received penetrating comments that have resulted in needed additions to various parts of this book. I also want to thank Susan G. Fenwick for critical suggestions on the rewriting of several passages, and David Horne for invaluable editoral help.

This work was first dedicated to my teacher Josef König, and is now dedicated to his memory.

F. M.-B.

New York City, 1980

*Fictive Discourse and the
Structures of Literature*

I. *The Logical Nature and Phenomenal Structure of Literary Narrative*

Structuralist studies of narrative usually discuss the general features of the fictional world, such as the sequence of actions, the nature and function of the characters, and the organization of objects and space; or they discuss the narrator's and the implied reader's role. This means that these studies presuppose the constitution of narrator, world, and implied reader as the objects of literary experience and critical analysis. From Vladimir Propp's *Morphology of the Folktale* to Roland Barthes' *S/Z,* and even beyond, the objectivity and the basic structure of the poetic cosmos are taken for granted. Nevertheless, the emergence of this imaginary objectivity—unquestioned by most theoreticians—is precisely the poetic-literary phenomenon par excellence.

In the present Chapter I investigate the constitution of narrative objectivity, describe its basic structure, and define the logical rules of fiction that make this objectivity possible.

1. *The Logical Characterization of Narrative Language*

Narration and Description: Species of the Same Genus of Speech

Underlying the ordinary use of the words "narration" and "description" are two notions that place these words in opposition (hence fundamentally conjoin them). Narration is the purely linguistic representation of change in particular persons, states of affairs, and circumstances, in the course of time. Description, on the other hand, is the representation of permanent, momentary, or recurring things, or events of short duration, in their unchanging aspects.

Therefore, since description, as opposed to narration, is reference to unchanging things, it is clear why the representation of generalities or abstractions is often termed, in a wider and derivative sense, "description," and never "narration." In this wider sense, the word "description" has gained currency in theoretical discussions. One hears of descriptions of essences as well as of landscapes, of experiences and semantic contents, and even of natural or historical occurrences. The name seems to apply to any representational discourse.

In another predominantly theoretical but more restricted sense, only the representation of particular or single things is termed description. One may speak of the description of the Battle of Waterloo, of the Taj Mahal, of President Nixon's last days in office. Thus, following this third usage, *description* is the common genus encompassing the two species *narration* and *description,* in the primary sense of these words with which we began.

The Narrative-Descriptive or "Mimetic" Sentence: Its Logical Definition

The initial and, in a sense, the overall subject of this study is not the difference between these two classes of representation but what they have in common as the narrative-or-descriptive sentence. Sentences such as "That afternoon, Peter left home," "The tree was tall, bare, and dry," "This is the house I was looking for," and "Those pencils are out of place" have concrete singularized entities as subjects—that is, as the objects about which the speaker is talking. They exemplify the type of sentence we are considering.

For obvious reasons, we must make a terminological decision and agree on a designation for this narrative-or-descriptive sentence, one that linguistically represents, or refers to, concrete individual beings. It would be ambiguous and misleading, as we have shown, to persist in using "description," even though it is often used in this sense. Given the traditional aesthetic-philosophical meaning of the term "mimesis," and the nature of the phenomenon in question, for which—as we shall see—the term is illuminating, henceforth we will designate this sentence a "mimetic sentence."

Mimetic discourse, whether narrative or descriptive, we will define as a species of linguistic formation essentially distinguished by the logical type of the basic sentence it contains, and not by stylistic excellence, ideal or affective contents, or association with particular literary forms. The mimetic sentence can be logically defined either as an *apophantic* (asseverative) sentence having a concrete singularized subject, or as a sentence carrying a "singular judgment" (in the traditional logical terminology of the division of judgments according to their "quantity")—that is, the judgment signified by a sentence like "Socrates is mortal."

Of course, the "particular" judgment of the traditional division ("Some Xs are Ys") is at times also essentially mimetic: in those cases when its subject is an aggregate of individuals or individualized groups—that is, in cases where it stands for a sum of singular judgments or is equivalent to a singular judgment with a collective subject. For example: "Some men came staggering along"—in other words, "Tom came staggering along, and Dick came staggering along, etc. . . ." Then, too, apparently "universal" or "general" judgments can be mimetic, as, for example, "All the children fell silent."

In these examples I use the past tense for greater clarity, in the absence of a context that makes their meaning univocal, so as to avoid the ambiguity inherent in the possibility of a truly particular or general use of these sentences in the present tense. But they could also be in the present tense without this precluding their singular or mimetic use. Altogether different is the nature of objective reference—that is, the manner of determining the subject of predication—in non mimetic, theoretical (whether universal or particular) judgments such as: "Primarily in their youth, some men feel immortal," or "All ills come to an end."[1]

(I emphasize the logical singularity of mimetic sentences and the individuality of their object-subjects, in order to preclude an inappropriate typification or classification of the persons, events, and circumstances described or narrated. The fundamental compass of narrative is a world of individuals. That the symbolic meaning or the general truth of what is represented may occasionally transcend this compass in ultimate significance must not be allowed to obscure this basic phenomenon. Moreover, the comprehension of such general meanings in the aesthetic sphere is possible only through attention to the basic individuality of the objects. Cervantes' Don Quixote is not basically a type or symbol, but an individual. As such he is a fictional entity and, despite the possible existence of a real model, has never existed—which, of course, raises an extremely difficult problem, that we must discuss elsewhere. The Quixotic type, on the other hand, *can* exist in real examples. Distinctions such as these are obvious, but they are nevertheless often ignored.)

As for the terms "apophansis" and "apophantic," they apply to any sentence that expresses a judgment, in the logical acceptance of the term "judgment." According to Aristotle in *De Interpretatione,* an apophantic sentence is one capable of being either true or false, or, more exactly, one in which either truth or falsehood inheres. Requests, questions, and exclamations are not of this type. In English there are various common expressions whose sense corresponds to apophantic discourse or apophantic sentence (such as "assertive," "affirmative," "declarative," "asseverative" sentences, or simply "statement"), but none does so precisely or unambiguously enough for our purposes. It would be easy to redefine some of these expressions in the requisite way and so convert them into technical terms. But I consider it preferable to avoid, whenever possible, making technical terms out of ordinary words, since this necessarily creates troublesome ambiguities.

"*Apophantic* sentence" seems, for these reasons, the best designation for sentences that assert states of affairs or circumstances as being facts, and are either true or false with respect to what is the case.

The Sentence as the Unit of Whole Speech and as Apophantic Content

Let us now introduce the (traditional) distinction between the apophantic sentence (a) as *the unit of whole speech* (the "sentence") and (b) as *pure apophantic content of the sentences of whole speech* (the "judgment," or "proposition," or "referential content"), whether or not the sentences in question are apophantic in a strict sense—that is, asseverative. Apophantic content is the essential determinant of asseverative sentences but does not constitute their only ingredient, since the sound pattern and the emotive connotations are also part of the sentence. Likewise, a judgment or a *proposition,* in the discourse of logi cians, is not the whole sentence but only its apophantic content. Traditionally, this content is also spoken of as the *representative, denotative,* or *referential* dimension of language. Nevertheless, in what follows we shall continue to use the terms "mimetic sentence" and "narrative-descriptive sentence," in addition to "mimetic content" and "singular apophantic content," and as their equivalents, despite the just-noted ambiguity of the first two terms and despite our continued use of them as referring to the whole sentence. The context should eliminate any chance of confusion. What has been said also applies *mutatis mutandis* to "mimetic discourse" and to "narrative-descriptive discourse": we will so designate both the whole narrative-descriptive discourse of the narrator and the content which is its essential determinant—that is, what is strictly *mimesis* or its *mimetic* part.

Obviously this distinction signals the abstract separation, within the compass of any sentence actually spoken, of two objectively discernible parts: one, the representative content, and the other, the phonic configuration and "affective" or "stylistic" content. (The legitimacy of such a distinction is easily shown by example. The sentences "There is no light in that street" and "That street is so very, very dark" carry—when adequately understood—the same apophantic content—the same fact settles in the same way the question of their truth or falsehood—in different phonic configurations and differing degrees of expressiveness or subjective manifestation.)

Apophansis and Mimesis

Mimesis is representation, and representation is the fundamental and, in a sense, exclusively the achievement—among the various kinds of discourse—of the apophantic logos. If exclamations, requests, or questions can put before the mind's eye not only the speaker's inwardness and the character of the intended listener, but also a represented objectivity, it is because of their implicit apophantic content. Thoroughly representative language is eminently apophantic. In essence, to narrate or to describe is to make asseverations with respect to individual beings or individualized groups—that is, to make a series of explicit or implicit singular judgments.

2. The Stratification of the Literary Work According to the Various Logical Kinds of Discourse

Mimetic Sentence and Mimetic Discourse as the Essence of the Narrative Work

Narratives with which we are familiar often contain many sentences that are other than the mimetic sentence we described in Section 1, above. There is no generic or a priori requirement that this should be so, but for that matter there is no reason either why these works should be pure singular apophansis. It just is a fact that they can contain different kinds of sentences.

Potentially, then, a narrative work has different logical spheres, and this raises the question of their structural relations and hierarchy. In any composition that can be properly called a narrative, narrative discourse—as we initially characterized it by opposition to descriptive discourse—will predominate (by tautological necessity). This discourse, like descriptive discourse, is fundamentally mimetic, in the sense already defined. Therefore, no work can be properly called narration unless the language that characterizes it as a whole, its predominant language, is an aggregate of mimetic sentences. A narrative work must be fundamentally asseverative speech about individu-

27

als. A study of the mimetic sentence is, therefore, a study of the essence of narration.

The Basic Structural Function of Mimetic Discourse as a Stratum of the Narrative Work

To our assertion that mimetic discourse is essential in any work properly called narration, we must add a determination of the basic function of such discourse in the structure of the narrative work—that is, of its relation to other discourse accompanying it.

Within the whole of a narrative work, mimetic (narrative-descriptive) discourse constitutes one stratum, the fundamental one, *as discourse of the narrator*. This stratum of language is distinguished in general terms from the other linguistic moments of which the narrator is the source because it is mimetic, and from the other discourses present (whether mimetic or not) because it is narrator's discourse. (We will presently give the distinction logical precision.)

Although this concept of the narrator's mimetic discourse abstracts from his speech the singular apophantic content, even within the unity of each sentence, and sets it apart from the other elements of whole speech, this singular apophantic content, or mimetic discourse, of the narrator is no mere abstraction. It is one stratum of the object that makes up the narrative work. Mimetic discourse *as a consistent whole* has a function in the structure of the work. The mimesis of the narrator provides the foundation for the dialogic and monologic discourses of the characters. The discourses of the characters have determinate meaning only to the extent that the sources and circumstances producing them are introduced by and in the mimetic base. It is always an explicit or implicit singular judgment of the narrator which determines the speech of a character as his ("Tom said: . . . ," for example). Moreover, it is mimetic discourse that puts the characters, potential speakers, before us in the first place. Thus the mimetic stratum carries the linguistic structure of the narrative composition; the different kinds of discourse are structurally organized and articulated on this base, and according to the implications of its contents.[2]

The Logical Difference between the Mimetic and the Other Linguistic Moments in the Narrator's Discourse

The other parts of language (those not mimetic discourse of the narrator) not only have a different structural function and place in the work, but also are of an intrinsically different logical nature—as we have already shown in part—from the narrator's mimetic discourse. (Of course, an approximate discrimination and characterization of these strata and structure is possible, in an intuitive-phenomenological way, without recourse to logical categories, but for precise comprehension, these categories are required.) The pertinent logical differentiae, pointed out above, refer, then, to the nonapophantic nature or the unsingularized subject of the non-narrative-descriptive discourse (or of the non-narrative-descriptive linguistic moments) of the basic speaker. This is the fundamental logical distinction within the speech of the narrator.

The Logical Difference between the Narrator's Speech and the Speech of the Characters

In contrast, our earlier differentiation between the mimetic discourse of the narrator and the other mimetic discourses (those of the characters), based as it was solely on the fact that the former is direct speech of the narrator, was not a logical distinction but a structural one. For a logical differentiation between the mimetic discourse of the narrator and the mimetic speech of the characters, we need, in addition, a fundamental logical concept: that of *truth* as an attribute of statements.

Potentially, the speech of the characters can exhibit all the possible forms of speech, since the characters can only be thought of unrestrictedly as potential speakers. Consequently, the possibility of a character delivering a mimetic sentence is inherent in the narrative work. If, because of its length and nature, the mimetic discourse of a character acquires the status of narration, the structure of the work is doubled (as in the "framed story"), and this replication may go on indefinitely (as happens with the characters' tales in *A Thousand and One Nights*), in which case the narrative base, with its structural properties, is each time passed along to the new mimetic discourse. Conversely, a sufficiently clear identifying mark or indication as to the origin of new sentences can draw the basic function back to the previously operative narrative strata, and, of course, even all the way back to the widest narrative frame of all—that is, the discourse of the fundamental narrator. These superimposed narratives, or narratives set one inside another, are all of the same logical nature but not of the same rank in a logical hierarchy, as we shall see; their difference is not merely their relative position in a multiple structure in which complete narratives are strata or units.

A superficial impression to the contrary, these pyramids of narrations do not constitute the narrative's greatest source of structural richness. They are no more than replicas of one and the same stratum, with its same logical and structural properties. It is, rather, *the speech of the characters that does not turn into narration*—and that, as dialogue or monologue, is set within a narrative discourse that retains its own fundamental role—which gives the work an additional logical dimension with a distinct nature of its own. For this possible speech of the characters is different in essence; it is not neatly and predominantly narrative-descriptive, like the narrator's speech, but a living mixture of all forms of natural discourse. In a dialogue, for example, the aphorism, or the sentence of generalized import, bulks just as large as the exclamation, the question, the request, or our familiar singular or mimetic sentence. In addition, the apophantic parts of the characters' speeches are—just as they would be in a real-life communicative situation—questionable, relative, perceived as open to doubt, sometimes giving the impression of truth, at other times an impression of falsehood or insincerity. The speech of the characters that remains ordinary speech and does not become narration has no more claim to credibility than that of speakers in the real world. This is not true of the narrator's discourse.

The mimetic sentences of the narrator are of a different power. Comprehension of a narrative requires in general—that is, whether it is a fictional or a nonfictional narrative—a particular receptivity to the narrator's words; we must extend to them a subtle form of fundamental credence (which does not preclude subsequent reflection, doubts, criticism, or counterproof, as in the case of nonfictional narrative, like historical writing) in order for the narrative to move forward, to unfold before our eyes, to become the image of a world. For the fundamental understanding of all narration, the requirement is that the mimetic sentences of the narrator, but not those of the characters, be accepted as true. If a conflict arises (contradiction, opposition, discrepancy) between the *singular* statements (i.e. statements concerning individuals) of the narrator and those of a character, the character is *at once* understood to be—intentionally or unintentionally—in error. The narrator's singular statements have logical preeminence.[3] This, then, is the essential logical difference between the narrator's mimetic sentences and those of any of the characters.

This logical validity, spontaneously accepted, is a functional characteristic of the narrative-descriptive stratum. The function can be (tacitly) delegated to the mimetic discourse of the characters, and this always takes place in the absence of any affirmations by the narrator regarding the individual aspect of the world to which the characters' narrative-descriptive sentences happen to refer. This often occurs with descriptions and accounts of events in dialogues or monologues, and particularly in the above-mentioned case of narration by a character, which then takes over all the functional-structural characteristics of the fundamental narration. But this delegation can only occur in the absence of the pertinent mimetic sentences of the basic narrator. This concept of logical preeminence or precedence, based upon the logical concept of truth as a sentence property, permits us to define further the different strata of mimetic language as, in each instance, not only distinct because of its respective speaker, but also logically different.

The pyramid of superimposed narrations has, then, the logical structure of a hierarchy based on precedence of validity.

Another Logical Distinction between the Mimetic and Other Apophantic Contents of the Narrator's Discourse

This concept of the spontaneous attribution of truth allows us to refine our distinction—regarding the narrator's discourse—between its mimetic content and its other linguistic moments. Only the narrator's mimetic sentences are accepted unquestioningly. By contrast, his other affirmations, his non-narrative-descriptive ones (generalizations, aphorisms, opinions, moral views—that is, all theoretical, universal and particular, non-mimetic judgments), receive, in an educated reading, adequate to a narrative work, only a qualified acceptance or a restrained acknowledgment. These affirmations exist on a different plane of logical validity. They are not privileged, like the mimetic ones; they are the narrator's own opinions and ideas. From the outset they are relative to his person and no image of a world flows from them, but instead an image of the narrator, inasmuch as these general judgments are offered as, and remain, judgments, thought, subjectivity, and language, act, expression. These sentences make manifest the personality of the narrator, and in this regard his universal apophansis is on the same plane and has the same function as the nonapophantic moments of his discourse.

We produce the following parodistic example in order to display the logical and aesthetic-structural planes of narrative:

Peter and John were strolling through the old part of the city and had just started down the avenue toward the river when Peter stuck out his arm and exclaimed: "There's another splendid temple!" "I don't see a temple or anything else splendid," John said dryly, continuing on in the same direction they had been heading.

Near at hand there was, in fact, a temple, a great bare, austere-looking mass. But Peter's continual exclamations of delight, inevitably followed by signs of youthful historical and artistic dilettantism, had put his rather uncommunicative companion out of sorts. Even the noblest of enthusiasms is as irritating as common drunkenness when too much in evidence.

"Let's catch that launch," John suggested suddenly, his voice harsh, as he gazed toward the river that was still some distance away. Peter immediately fell into step beside him and they hurried on together.

The narrator's sentence about the existence of the temple on the street down which the characters are walking resolves the contradiction in what they say, since it represents the truth of the matter and determines the constitution of the object. At this particular place in this particular city there is, quite simply, a temple. To question this is to refuse to read the narrative as fiction. On the other hand, the narrator's general observation about excessive expressions of enthusiasm receives only qualified acceptance, not because in itself it may fail to convince us, but because, in the aesthetic attitude of reading, it only matters that this is an opinion of the narrator, and so his personality, with which we are already acquainted through his way of telling a story, is thrown into even sharper relief. In the reading game of imaginally projecting a world and a narrator, there is no room for reflection on the truth of universal judgments, nor any need to give them a feigned credence in order to experience the full sense of the narrative. Finally, the implicit affirmation in John's last speech, that there is a launch to be seen, although spoken by a character, takes on all the logical and constitutive strength of the fundamental stratum, and so determines what the landscape shall be as long as there is no affirmation by the narrator concerning this possible aspect of the fictional world.

3. The Logical Privilege of Mimetic Discourse as an Enabling Rule of the Experience of Narrative

The spontaneous attribution of validity to the narrator's mimetic discourse, and the corresponding hierarchy of logical priority, are a constitutive rule of narrative as object—in Kantian terms, a *transcendental* form or principle of the comprehension or experience of narration. The general objective of all narrative (literary or not) is to place a real or fictional sector of the world before the eyes of our imagination, to cause us by means of language to imagine the narrated circumstances. And the sentence taken to be true is the one that makes the imagined world possible. Such a sentence, by establishing the image it projects as something that *is* or *has been* thus and so, makes immediately present an aspect of the world's configuration. To attribute truth to a sentence and so give credence to the speaker is to project (in imagination) an aspect of the world. If accepted with reservation, the mimetic sentence is incapable of this function; the image it proposes remains uncertain and insubstantial because it does not receive the full projection of the mind.[4]

In narrative that is specifically literary, defined as one aimed at *fulfillment within its own boundaries,* the validity attributed to the narrator's mimetic discourse is maximal, absolute. Thus literary narrative unresistingly unfolds as a vision of the world. This often enlightened and serious game of constructing worlds formed of narrative images requires, as a law of the quasi-mechanics of illusion, that the narrator receive our unqualified credence. If this rule of the game is disobeyed, there is no (literary) object. Of course, this credence is given only with a more or less clear ironic awareness of this artifice of the imagination. Strictly speaking, such an unreserved outpouring of faith is possible only because it operates within the awareness that what is narrated is fiction. This proves that the very fictitiousness of the narrated object, as the enabling condition of an unreserved ironic credulity, is the required instrument for an uninhibited narrative image; the very possibility of literature, in a strict sense, lies in its fictiveness.

The narrative world is constituted before us just as the narrator, in mimetic sentences, tells us it is. Mimetic discourse determines its configuration. We have here *in nuce* a Kantian deduction of transcendental forms of literary experience: the rules of literary reading, such as the ironic acceptance of the absolute truth of the narrator's mimetic apophansis, are conditions of the possibility of the object called literature.

It is easy to see how the above-described logical system of literary narrative opens the technical-stylistic possibility of the so-called "unreliable narrator." To construct such a mode of representation it is sufficient to use a secondary narrator whose mimetic sentences are deviant from the corresponding mimetic sentences of the basic narrator. Or, making the basic narrator himself unreliable, to create a perceptible difference between the impression of the events derived by the reader solely from the mimetic moments of the basic narrator's discourse, and the view of the same events present in the non-mimetic components of the same discourse (that is, in the narrator's general judgments, commentaries, expressions of feelings, etc.).

This game of unreliability, inconsistency, and ambiguity can indeed reach inside the mimetic sentence itself; it occurs because of the difference between "determinant" and "modifying" predicates—a distinction taken from Husserl and developed by Josef König in his *Sein und Denken*.[5] This distinction opposes predicates that designate the more objective properties of things, states, relations (such as designations of movements, colors, shapes, positions, etc.), and the more subjective qualities (such as mood, expression of character, values). This difference is perceptible in a sentence like the following: ''Winterstone continued handing food and medicine to the wounded men and children, repugnantly perseverant, disgustingly devoted, obscenely pious.'' No admissible reading of this fictional sentence as part of a literary narrative would question the ''fact'' that Winterstone handed food and medicine to the wounded men and children. What is unreliable or, say, doubtful is the simultaneously posited negative character or value of this action.[6]

4. The Phenomenal Strata of the Narrative Work

Mimetic Alienation or Transparency

We are ready to take a further step toward comprehending the structure of the narrative work. A phenomenological contemplation of the mimetic stratum is in order, now that it has received a logical determination and its structural function and ontic necessity have been presented or suggested.

In entertaining mimetic discourse as absolutely true, we put aside any reflection on the sentences themselves and turn our attention to the world whose determinate configuration the sentences narrate and describe, and whose being is unequivocally established by the truth of the sentences.

Our gaze does not pause before this language as before something that has and retains the character of language—as it does when confronted with the non-mimetic sentences of the narrator and the non-narrative speech of the characters. Mimetic language is as though transparent; it does not interpose itself between us and the things of which it speaks. The non-narrative-descriptive parts of the narrator's discourse refer us back to his presence, since they remain obvious as language and are *his* language, his acts *qua* narrator, his perceptible subjectivity, whereas mimetic discourse directs us toward world-things. Stated more precisely, we do not encounter the mimetic stratum as a linguistic stratum. We only encounter it as *world;* as *language* it disappears. Its representation of the world is an imitation of it that results in their confusion, their identification. *Mimetic discourse mimetizes itself as world. It alienates itself and becomes its own object.*

Understood in this way, the concept of mimesis neither implies nor precludes fidelity to an empirical reality. To *imitate* with words, in this basic sense, one formally prior to the Aristotelian notion, is to have the words become a world, which these words carry as their apophantic-mimetic potentiality. This potentiality of the words is realized when they disappear as words and become the things meant, or, more precisely, images of the things meant, their imaginary presence. Subsequent to the apophantic-mimetic actualization of these sentences is their potential function of descriptively aiming at real objects—that is, their possible development in, and their application to, the real world. At this second level the sentence previously accepted as true is discovered to be in fact true or false. The imitation will then be faithful or inadequate, whether in a particular sense (adequate or not in reference to the singular events it then represents) or in a general way (the realistic or unrealistic nature of the kind of world given in images). But it will never be any less an "imitation," in the basic sense, no matter how inexact and false as to singular fact it is, or how unrealistic in regard to the universe it implicitly designs. Its being an imitation is prior to this distinction. (Croce points to this phenomenon when he states that intuition is prior to the distinction of real and unreal.)[7] In literature the imaginal imitation has its end in itself, as is often said in ambiguous and vague terms, meaning that it is to be valued not for its possible applicability to particulars in the real world, but for itself as an image of the totality of experience, real and/or possible. Hence, it does not matter to the reader of fiction whether literary mimesis may subsequently find historiographic employ—and the narrative be read as an historical document: this is beyond the aesthetic sphere and beyond aesthetic interest. Literary imitation is radically fiction. To imitate, in this most general sense, is to make the image of a *world* (irrespective of whether this image imitates any individual, real things or reproduces them, or imitates our world in general, or only *a* world). *Poetic* imitation must be, like all imitation, faithful to the idea of *a* world, for this is a necessary condition of all images insofar as they are images of something, and faithful to the idea of *our* world only insofar as they are images made in our language.

Clearly, the phenomenon of mimesis that is evinced in these observations is related to, but more radical than, the one envisioned in the traditional Aristotelian notion. Aristotle's concept of mimesis (as we infer from his examples in the *Poetics*) supposes empirical models, either individuals (as in portraits) or universal types (as in the representation of men and women, young and old, good and bad, etc.). According to the philosopher, as is well known, poetry must be faithful not to individual facts but to the general nature of our world. This is why, in Aristotle's concept, poetry is "more philosophical than history." But, as we see, its philosophical import may be even greater than that.

What I indicate, then, when I speak of the mimetic function of singular apophantic discourse is the phenomenon of the emergence of imaginary concrete objectivity from the appropriate understanding of words. It is another matter whether this imaginary objectivity, in its turn, imitates singular or generic empirical models, or creates previously unseen kinds of imaginary entities; both are different, and in a sense subsequent, possibilities of basic mimesis. This is not to suggest, however, that just anything could arise as an imaginary projection of the singular apophantic contents of sentences. Either the semantic boundaries of the language used or the general categories of objectivity will predetermine the nature of the imaginary construct: the represented entity—no matter how free of empirical models—will have number, relative position in its own space or time, parts and properties, and other a priori determinations of the transcendental constitution of individual beings. Even if these determinations (as is partly the case in contemporary literature) are intentionally unstable, ambiguous, or simply negated, they will be there in their negativity, in their suspended virtuality.

The fundamental relation of mimesis is not the relation of imaginary appearances to their empirical subjects, but the conversion of the stuff of thought into the appearance of images (of persons, things, spaces, events, entities), the conversion of transparent significations into opaque objectivities. Only upon this basis, and secondarily, is imitation of this or of that—or its alternative, "free" imagination—possible. Mimetic sentences, in my terminology, are the ones whose meanings can become concrete, singular objects for the mind. "All men are mortal" cannot provide that transformation. "Socrates is only a man, not one of the immortal gods," can.

The Logical Stratum of the Mimetic as a Phenomenal Stratum

The mimetic stratum is not, then, simply a logical level (a mere abstraction), nor simply a stratum distinguishable by virtue of its fundamental structural functions, but rather a perceptible entity, a discretely perceptible phenomenal presence. The mimetic stratum is the image of what is narrated. It must be understood, however, that in a certain sense the mimetic stratum *is* an abstraction, as we hinted earlier. First of all, it is clearly an entity abstracted from the general unity of the narrator's discourse. The total discourse of the narrator is obviously not one stratum, but the entire work. (What the characters say is included as parts of his discourse, specifically as the complements of sentences of the narrator which, implicitly or explicitly, introduce them.) But the abstract nature of the mimetic stratum, of mimetic discourse and mimetic sentences, becomes especially clear when one considers that in the very unity of each sentence which the narrator speaks, the mimetic part is only the singular apophantic content. This means that everything in the sentence spoken which is grammatical structure or affective content or phonic pattern, and so forth, lies outside, separate from, the mimetic stratum. Therefore, what is involved here is eminently an abstraction. Faced, however, with the perceptible presence of this stratum as a phenomenal unity, we stated previously that it was not a "mere" abstraction. As opposed to a mere abstraction or artificial conceptual construction, the type of abstraction of the mimetic sentence can be called a *natural* abstraction, for the detachment and separation of the mimetic stratum from the linguistic strata proper (that of the narrator and that of the speech of the characters), occurs spontaneously and necessarily in the thing that is the literary work, as though by a law of its own structure. As an essential moment in the development of its being and meaning, every explicitly or implicitly mimetic sentence neatly divides, on being understood by a reader or listener, into a mimetic content that becomes transparent and disappears from the linguistic plane, and the remainder, consisting of idiomatic form and expressed subjectivity that persist as expression, as language.

The Remaining Logicophenomenal Strata

The speech of the narrator as linguistic figure plus subjectivity, then, constitutes a properly linguistic stratum that is perceived as such. This stratum is constituted by the series of his narrative acts. This stratum is, therefore, the narrator himself as narrator, as subjectively engaged in narration. The sounds we intuit in the aesthetic apprehension of the narrative are his narrative voice.[8] And the fact that this is a discrete stratum of the narrative work means that the narrating subjectivity is objectified, is a part of the work. Thus in speaking of the narrator we have not been speaking of the author's real person.

In narrative discourse there are, at times, mimetic sentences that refer not to the narrated world, but to the narrator as such: precisely to him as an instance of someone *narratively confronting* that world (and, on occasion, confronting himself as one character among others). These mimetic sentences are not transmuted into part of that world but, obviously, into the narrator himself. They remain, therefore, in the linguistic stratum, not as language or as expressed inwardness, but as an image of the basic speaker—as representation, not expression.[9]

The only mimetic sentences that continue to be perceptible as language are those spoken by the characters—when they do not actually engage in fully developed narration or description. Because we are precluded (by the rules of the game) from an unreserved acceptance of their apophantic content, we hold these sentences in a sphere of pure intentionality, their primitive and original sphere of language. In the logical-structural perspective we have adopted in these pages, the dialogic-monologic language of the characters constitutes the third stratum of the narrative work. This is, properly speaking, a linguistic stratum, but in a sense different from the, stratum of the narrator. The stratum of the narrator is not of necessity purely linguistic, since it potentially includes mimesis of the narrator himself, derived from enunciations about him as narrator. It consists basically, however, only of the idiomatic-grammatical aspects of what he says (linguistic forms, sound) and of subjectivity that is not *said* but made manifest through the sentences spoken—what is expressed stylistically, or by means of represented or mimetic contents. Only part of the fundamental being of language, then, is displayed on this, the narrator's, level; an essential determinant of this level is that it lacks singular apophantic content as the immanent signification of the sentence—that is, it lacks whole, unsplit mimetic sentences, mimetic sentences that have not become mimetically transparent. In contrast, the whole being of language is displayed in the stratum of what the characters say. On this level, whole natural language is perceived as an object; it is one thing among others in the narrated world, inserted there as an act of the characters; yet it is a discrete stratum and not simply part of the mimetic stratum, because *as words* it is an entity without *aspectual* (limited) presence—in contrast to all other things in the narrated world. Instead, each word that is actually understood is always given in its entirety. Words spoken by the characters in dialogues or monologues are not narration-description that has become mimetically objectified, not representation in language, but something present in and of itself.

Mimetic sentences, in the sense we have defined, are found in all three strata. But only the mimetic sentences of the narrator actually become mimetically transparent and disappear, because only they are transmuted by the attribution of truth.

The preceding observations refer expressly to narrative in general and, occasionally and also expressly, to literary narrative in particular. Therefore, what has been defined is a fundamental type of linguistic work, of linguistic form, of discourse. The historical literary *genres* do not correspond to pure forms of language (such as narration, description, mimetic discourse, theoretical discourse, or pure general apophansis, exclamatory language, imperative language, etc.), nor do they correspond to pure structures, such as the one described here for the narrative work. The novel, for example, does not necessarily exhibit a pure narrative structure. At times it is predominantly descriptive or largely presented in dialogue, or given as the monologue of a character (for instance through the techniques of interior monologue or stream of consciousness), or completely as dialogue, or in epistolary form (dialogic narration). This means that the genre of the novel is not of necessity narrative in a linguistic sense. The exact determination of the concept of narrative makes possible a better understanding of these diverse phenomena. What we have found in our exposition thus far which is essential to the novelistic genre is that it is a purely linguistic mimetic fiction, having as its base, in common with all literature, the convention that pertinent, explicit or implicit, mimetic sentences be taken as true.

II. *The Structure of Linguistic Signification: Semantic Dimensions of Language*

Since the late forties, the structure of narrative and of the literary work in general has usually been deduced from the model of the functions and relations of the linguistic sign proposed by Karl Bühler.[1] More recently, Roman Jakobson's model of linguistic communication has served this same purpose. Wolfgang Kayser was influential in the spread of Bühler's schema as the fundamental structure of narrative. In our preceding analysis these same categories were implicit. We now turn to specific consideration of the functions of language. In Chapter III we will attempt to develop a concept of the structure of the literary work that follows from our own conception of the structure of linguistic signification.

In contrast to Chapter I (limited to narrative discourse), the study of the semantic functions and dimensions of language undertaken here is intended to have an unrestrictedly general applicability; it aims at a conception of the language of literature and of literature as language. Narrative in particular, along with lyric poetry and drama, will be the subject of a final clarification in Chapter III.

5. Bühler's Schema: A Model of Language as Organon

Bühler's schema contains a nucleus of insight together with some fundamental defects. More exactly stated, his schema fails to conceptualize adequately the insight from which it originates. It helps to see many things, but it obscures many others. We begin with a critical revision of Bühler's linguistic model. This requires a full awareness of the insights that the theory already contains. First, we will reexamine its achievements, and then describe the incongruities between the intuition of the phenomenon and this, its classic conceptualization. Lastly, we will attempt to set forth a more adequate conceptual schema.

In my usage *linguistic sign* essentially refers to a sentence or sentences as actually spoken in a communicative situation: as units or instances of speech (*parole*). This is the object of Bühler's model and the main subject of Husserl's "First Investigation." We will occasionally use the term "linguistic sign" in a different, clearly distinguishable sense, understanding in this latter case, with Saussure, an element of the language (*langue*), a potentiality that is actualized in sentences, a possibility that is always at the speaker's disposal. But we will resort to this second terminological usage only in referring to an actual sign, in order to explain its semantic structure. Examples of signs as units of speech are sentences like "That's the book I've been looking for," "What a terrible morning!" "Hand me that pencil," etc., taken as actually spoken in an actual situation of interhuman communication, wherein such sentences constitute the fundamental linguistic level (that is, not taken as examples included in a discussion of grammar or the like). (Husserl's preferred objects of reference, in developing his investigation, are sentences of the type "the three perpendiculars of a triangle intersect in a point," when actually spoken and seriously meant.) In recent years this notion of linguistic sign has become widespread, for instance in *Textlinguistik*.[2]

The elements of this model (in addition to the sign itself) are (a) the *speaker* (narrator), (b) the *listener* (audience, reader), and (c) the *events* or *things* (objects described, narrated story). The sign, the linguistic configuration, is the instrument of mediation between these three elements. The relations between the sign and each of the three elements constitute the sign's signifying functions, or its semantic dimensions.[3] (1) The sign's function as determined by the relation between the speaker and the sign (his speech) is termed *expressive*,[4] inasmuch as it externalizes the speaker's subjectivity. In this dimension, the sign is called a "symptom" or "index." (2) As a "symbol," the sign *represents* its referents ("it stands for them," we might say). (3) In relation to the addressee, the sign has an intentional effect, that is, an *appellative* function, and under this aspect it deserves the name "signal." Every complete language situation necessarily includes *someone* who says *something* to *someone else*. This is Bühler's schema of the functions of language.

Bühler asserts that the essential ingredients of his model are indicated by Plato in the *Cratylus*. We may add that Aristotle, too, in his *Rhetoric* (1358a,b), enumerates the elements of the language situation. Bruno Snell, who some years ago revised this schema, finds it prefigured in Dilthey.[5] It is not difficult to find it here and there; in fact it enjoys wide currency. With certain variations, Friedrich Kainz, Charles Morris, and Bertrand Russell have all worked with this linguistic model (to mention only authors whose work we will consider in this regard). Roman Jakobson's modification and extension of the model will be discussed in Appendix IV.

6. *The Varieties of Sign That Husserl Distinguishes*

Husserl, in his "First Investigation" on meaning, has shown that speech is at once sign-index and sign-symbol—that is, there are *two* related yet distinct senses in which speech can be properly termed a sign.[6] The word "symbol" does not appear in this part of his text (Husserl places "index," "indicium," "signal," "indication"—*Anzeichen, Signal,* and *Anzeige*—in opposition to "expression" and "meaningful sign"—*Ausdruck,* and *bedeutsames Zeichen*). But the pertinent concept is the same. What a speech is an indicium of, what is "made manifest" or "manifested" (*kundgegeben*) through the speech, is the speaker's subjectivity, especially the psychic acts that give meaning to (verbal) expressions. In opposition to this, what a speech means or actually *says* is an ideal meaning, an objective unit of thought, something in essence transcending the subjectivity of the speaker. If, in authentic discourse, I say: "The three perpendiculars of a triangle intersect in a point," what is said and meant is precisely this, that the three perpendiculars of a triangle intersect in a point, a proposition from geometry, an objective something that is one and the same in every situation in which these words occur authentically. On the other hand, what is manifested, what the words reveal, or are an *index of,* is the speaker's (concrete, individual, *hic et*

48

nunc) act of so judging, and by so judging of giving that meaning to the spoken words.

Obviously, the two dimensions of the linguistic sign distinguished in this way differ not only in the nature of the object they introduce into the sphere of communication, but even more profoundly in their respective modes of introducing it. The meant object is *said,* represented by symbols, intentionally aimed at. The externalized subjectivity (perceptible in inadequate "external" perception, according to Husserl) is not said, is not the object of words, and is not represented by them, but instead is merely revealed, as by a kind of symptom.

What is not said but made manifest, then, as opposed to what is said and represented, is the object of a specific and discrete mode of signification (of "putting on view," of making known, of communicating). This is how we interpret Husserl's notion of meaning, using his terminology, as well as Bühler's, and thereby demonstrating the fundamental correspondence of these approaches.

7. Bally: The System of the "Expressive" Resources of Language

Charles Bally, in his pioneering work on stylistics, went to great lengths to demonstrate that the system of language (*langue*) is not constituted solely to serve "logical" ends (and with his usage this means, precisely, "representative" ends), but also to serve in the "expression" of affect and volition (generally: of the subjectivity of the speaker) and in linguistic action upon the hearer.[7] His stylistics is a study of the general "expressive" resources (in Bally's terminology "expressive" resources means resources for "making manifest"—Husserl, Bühler—and for "appellation"—Bühler) of a linguistic community. His conception of language as an organ of *life* constitutes a wider view of language than do the distinctions made by Husserl: not only are the psychic acts that give meaning to words made manifest through these same words, but so are the speaker's attitude, situation, condition, and inner self. In addition, the effective, coercive valences of language are also incorporated in his theory. So it can be said that Bally's stylistics is the study of the elements of language which exist as tools of the non-representative-symbolic dimensions of speech—that is, the "expressive" and "appellative" dimensions.

8. *Recapitulation*

Neither the full implications of Bühler's model, nor its fundamental correspondence with, and complementation by, other contemporary theories of language, nor, in general, the revelation of linguistic phenomena brought about by these theoretical insights, have been adequately assimilated by our critical tradition. Yet enrichment of our view of language, as well as a refinement of its conceptualization, presupposes a correct reexperiencing of these insights.

Each single speech is a sign, then, not just in one but in three distinct senses of the word "sign." This is to be understood literally: it is not a question of different, simultaneous dimensions of a linguistic *reference* (as in an intentional ambiguity). Rather, we are speaking of essentially different ways of being a sign or of having meaning, of distinct *sui generis* semantic dimensions. (Neither Husserl nor Bühler goes so far as to say that these different concepts of sign correspond to species of a common genus;[8] and since, on the other hand, no case can be made for this being merely an instance of synonymy, it may legitimately be supposed that this difference in the ways of being a sign is a *radical* one, in the terminological sense given this word by Josef König. In König's view it would be a question not simply of different kinds of signs, but of signs that *as signs* are different.)[9]

These considerations of and allusions to the history of the theory that Bühler refurbished serve to highlight what seems to me one of its greatest and most often misunderstood discoveries—namely, the phenomenon of different, simultaneous *semantic modes* of speech. Now we can initiate our critique of Bühler's model. First we will review its salient incongruities (together with a discussion of some of the fundamental points of Kainz's critique of it), and then, with the phenomenon itself before us, we will proceed to a basic revision of Bühler's schema, a revision that will enable us to understand and go beyond the several shortcomings we will have indicated in the course of the discussion.

9. *Incongruities in Bühler's Model*

The Elements of the Model

To begin with, it is inappropriate to use "index" or "symptom" (in opposition to "symbol" and "signal") in general to designate the sign in its relation to the speaker. Clearly the speaker not only *expresses* his inner self and being through unintended symptoms, but he often also *speaks about* them; for example, he directly refers to his psychic states—that is, he represents or symbolizes them in the same way he represents and symbolizes the objects around him. Sentences like "I'm sad," "I can't remember that," "My foot hurts," or simply "I'm bald" (notice that the first element of the model is the *speaker,* without qualification or restriction) signify what they say in exactly the same way as the sentences "That rose is red," "Pedro is an athlete," etc. That the speaker is the subject of such sentences in no way implies a *sui generis* semantic relation that is different from representation. A semantic relation of sign to speaker is not necessarily a new dimension of signification, differing from that which in general links the sign to the things described. The speaker is an object to which he can refer as to any other. Therefore, it would be not only a misuse of ordinary language, but an unfounded technical use of the word to say, for example, of a sentence like "I'm sad" that it is simply an index or symptom of the speaker's state of sadness. Of course, a sentence like this, when actually spoken, is also an index or symptom of the speaker's state (of his judging it to be a fact that he is sad); and it can even be, in addition, through its modulation and tone, an index of precisely the state of sadness that the sentence itself describes or represents; but this in no way means that it ceases to be the representation or symbol or description of that state of sadness. What is said in such a sentence is that the subject is sad, irrespective of what may be expressed or made manifest by means of the sentence. Confusion over this point is frequent. Bertrand Russell states: "If I exclaim 'I am hot!,' the fact indicated is a state of myself, and is the very state that I *express.*"[10] "Indicated" in Russell's terminology is equivalent to "represented" in Bühler's. The fact represented by Russell's example-sentence is, in truth, the speaker's state of being hot, but much more, and something in essence quite different, is "expressed": the fact of the speaker's *judging* that he is hot, and his *wanting to say so,* and his *saying so,* together with all that these facts imply as manifestations of attitude, condition, and character.

In general, the representation of an inner state "expresses," fundamentally, not the represented state but the act of reflecting on it and communicating it. (It must always be remembered that we use the word "expression"—as do Russell and most of the authors referred to, with the obvious exception of Husserl's use of *Ausdruck*—in a technical sense (corresponding to Jakobson's term "emotive" function) as designating the mode of linguistic signification that stands in opposition to representation and "appellation" (or "conation," in Jakobson's terminology). In one of the *ordinary* uses of this word it can be said, of course, that "I am hot!" expresses the condition of being hot. But in this usage the word signifies a different concept; it is, strictly speaking, a different word.)

Naturally, the above applies, mutatis mutandis, to the relation of the sign to the hearer. The sign can be a symbol of the hearer, can describe him, or represent him. Additionally, it can be termed a "signal" insofar as it elicits a particular conduct from him. But it would be capricious not to recognize that "You will get cigarettes," for example, said in the appropriate situation, in addition to expressing a wish and functioning as a signal in search of a reaction, is related to the hearer and his conduct *in the same way* (even if, here, prospectively) as any description is to its object.

That is, a linguistic sign may entertain "representative" relations with each element of the schema, and can therefore be a "symbol" in respect to each one of them. All three elements are potentially things that can be spoken about. Even the sign itself can be the object of a self-reference.

This first criticism may seem to touch upon superficial or simply terminological aspects of the model. Its consequences are nevertheless considerable. It makes clear that it is not simply the relation of sign to speaker or hearer that generates modes of signification other than the representative-symbolic one. Furthermore, it shows that much of what belongs to the speaker and to the hearer (physical aspects and other properties) can never stand in any but a descriptive-symbolic relation to the linguistic sign. We must face, then, the problem of determining *what* is actually related to the sign in semantic functions or dimensions that are not representative, precisely *what* is linguistically expressed without being said, and *which facets* of the hearer are related to the sign without being named or described by it. In other words, *the schema must be reworked by redefining the elements in terms of the modes of signification, instead of the reverse.* What is immediately given here is the sign's three-dimensionality. We have just as original an experience of the expressive and appellative phenomena as we do of the phenomenon of representation; we are just as familiar with linguistic symptoms and signals as we are with linguistic symbols. Therefore, our interpretation of the appropriate relations must be derived from these phenomena. In this sense the model would be correct if the elements were: in place of "speaker," *inner self or mode of being made manifest in speech;* in place of "hearer," *reaction or change caused by speech;* in place of "objects and states of affairs," *that which is spoken about.* (The "change caused by speech" should be taken in a broad sense so as to include, as is natural, the psychic change that constitutes the acts of hearing and understanding. The outer limits of such a change, as Dámaso Alonso says in *Poesía española,* are impossible to determine.[11] For our purposes, as regards the phenomenon of the appellative dimension of speech, we will define it as the *immediate and complete* change produced by the sign and its meaning.)

Our new terms make clear, and susceptible to conceptualization, the important type of communication of someone speaking to himself, without our having to say, rather inexactly and paradoxically, that in this case the speaker is also the hearer (even if this turn of phrase is not entirely wrong). *All* actual speech has the three dimensions of meaning. When thoroughly understood, this proves how erroneous is Kainz's radical distinction between the "dialogic" and the "monologic" functions of language.[12] In the phenomena remarked on by Kainz, it is rather a question of the same functions *in different communicative situations,* in which they acquire different additional meanings. Furthermore, the often-mentioned phenomenon of "dominance" of one function over the others can also, in certain cases referred to by Bühler, be subjected to a fundamental ordering grounded in the basic types of communicative situation: communication aimed at information, communication aimed at self-integration, and active-practical communication. (In this respect, see our distinctions in Chapter III regarding epic, lyric poetry, and drama.) It is wrong to assert that these three dimensions are only the maximum exercise of the possible linguistic functions, and that (as Bühler believes, par. 2) the schemas that correspond to other types of language acts can be obtained by their "reduction." Bertrand Russell also asserts that there are sentences lacking one or two functions, but an analysis of the communicative situation demonstrates the contrary, as we shall see.

At the same time we must caution against the frequent suggestion that the three functions of language derive from the three "faculties of the soul," feeling, thinking, and desiring. (Kainz makes fun of this weakness for certain vague and grandiloquent formulas, but he fails to warn against the dangers of this one.) It is clear, on reflection, as far as the contents of the semantic dimensions are concerned, that one can *speak of* phenomena belonging to all three orders (make them the object of the representative function), just as one can *make* them *manifest* (make them the content of expression) by saying something about something else, and, finally, that one can also elicit them as effects of speech (making them the result of appellation). Especially does it seem an unnecessary narrowing of vision to limit the region of expression to what is "affective" or "emotive" (as I. A. Richards' and R. Jakobson's terminologies suggest we do). On the other hand, taken as a mode of signification, it is true that "representing" is (a form of) thinking; nevertheless, we cannot say that "expressing" is feeling, or that appellation is desire.

The Interdetermination of the Elements

A second incongruence of Bühler's model is that it sees the functions of language as mutually independent.[13] In fact, in this model, expression, representation, and appellation appear to be different independent powers of the sign. Reflection does not support such a view. Not only the sign itself, but also the character of what is represented as well as the character of the intentional appellation are all unintended means by which the speaker's inner self is given expression. Similarly, what is expressed and what is represented are both factors of appellation. For example, if someone shouts "A snake!" both the expressed fear and the mention of the object are constitutive elements of the appellative force of this particular linguistic act. But on a more profound level, the rigorous and, for matters of communication, decisive interdependence of the semantic dimensions is most clearly shown by the fact that the representative dimension can be achieved only through the expressive dimension. This was shown, *in nuce*, by Husserl: I understand the speaker (that is, I know *what* he *says*), only if I sense his concrete (actual, present) intention by means of the index that his words are of this intention. Essentially, what is made manifest is the actual signifying intention of the speaker, and this actual intention is the bearer of the intended representation (Husserl's "meaning"—*Bedeutung*), just as, in general, the individual is the bearer of the characteristics of his species.[14]

In point of fact, the three dimensions, in a complex process of mutual determination, enrich one another with successive strata. A phenomenology of communication is required to discern this network of the communicative situation, which in practice is always hidden from view.[15]

There exist, then, *direct* or *immediate* expression and appellation, which are products of the simple actualization of the "expressive" (Bally) conventions of the language (for example, imperative and exclamatory forms, etc.), as well as *indirect* expression and appellation, the latter produced by means of representation and by the respective other dimension. We may say, directly, "Get out of here!," or, indirectly, "I want to be alone now," and again, "Disgusting!," or, "That sight is unpleasant," and so on.

The Immanent Semantic Dimensions

The last incongruence of Bühler's model that we will discuss—the most subtle of all—becomes apparent the moment we pursue the previous one a little farther. Of course, our logical sense immediately perceives, albeit somewhat vaguely, that the triplet "symptom-signal-symbol" is imperfect, that it confuses different levels and blurs relevant differences. But in order to obtain a correct theoretical explication of what are at first only impressions, we must submit the model's implications to a careful analysis. This will be our immediate task: a critique of the model that will expose its aporia. Then we will return to the phenomenon itself and evolve a new theory.

Kainz has criticized this terminological triplet, but his reasons are not convincing.[16] According to him, Bühler, with his terminology, goes against the fundamental fact that language is *in essence* symbolic. According to Kainz the linguistic sign is a symbol in all three of its functions: it is an expressive symbol, a representative symbol, and an appellative symbol. In none of its functions does he consider language to be an altogether different type of sign. Of course, this stand is in keeping with his previous decision to exclude conceptually from language proper all that is not the symbolic representation of objects. But such a conception reduces the phenomenon of language well beyond its natural limits and disregards equally essential aspects of human speech. Actually, it returns the vision of language to the limited scope it enjoyed before the liberating work of Croce, Vossler and his school, Bally, and, in the aspect discussed, Husserl. In other words, Kainz ignores a much richer intuition of the phenomenon, one that is already an historical acquisition. It is precisely the basic merit of Bühler's model to have incorporated the nonsymbolic (symptomatic and signaling) modes of the linguistic sign, and in so doing to have circumscribed its specifically expressive and causative projections. In this way the whole realm of human speech is exposed to reflection.

In Kainz's conception the three semantic dimensions become merely different directions of signification—that is, their difference is based solely on the diverse spheres to which they are directed, each one of these spheres being the potential object of a symbolic reference. But for Kainz the reference itself is always of the same nature, in other words, the mode of signifying the given sphere is the same in each case. This, I think, collapses the schema of the functions of speech. Nothing remains except a principle of classification of the possible objects of speech, deduced from the three elements of the communicative relationship, and, in addition to this, a tripartite division of the function of linguistic *representation*. (In keeping with this, Kainz replaces the name of the function "representation"—*Darstellung*—with "report," "understanding," "information"—*Bericht, Verständigung, Information*—and reserves the term "representation" for the essential nature of all language. The level of the functions of speech and the level of the kinds of speech acts, and even that of the forms of discourses, are thus confused.)

In point of fact, it is true that linguistic *representation* has not only these three directions, but also, in a sense, the three possible functions— that is, it has them to the extent that the other dimensions (including a replication of the representative one itself) can be added, as additional aspects to a basic nucleus, to the representative dimension. The functions thus become (external) relations of the linguistic symbol. The insight that underlies Kainz's conception provides a clue to the fundamental incongruence of

Bühler's model. Despite his disregard of the other semantic dimensions, which leads him to make unwarranted generalizations, Kainz's criticism inadvertently shows that semantic functions or dimensions can be superimposed on one another. That is, representation can be the fundament of the other two and of its own duplicate. A representation can be the medium that carries an expression, an additional representative function, and an appellation. For example, the representation contained in a sentence like "The land is parched, the garden withered, and the homestead vacant," carries within it an expressive power: what is said reveals the speaker as someone who speaks precisely of these things and, therefore, of things of this kind, that he relates these sorts of things with one another, that he is impressed by them, etc. In addition, this representation, borne by the sentence (type) in each and every one of its actualizations (tokens), is what makes it possible in a given situation for a determinate speaker to *mention* (and this is the additional representative function) the particular land, garden, and homestead that he and his interlocutor have before them. And this in turn makes possible a concretely defined appellation vis-à-vis the listener, since in being spoken to he is necessarily urged to take in the situation described. Other examples that show clearly how representation can be the medium of expression would be the following: to speak of intimate things may reveal candor, to dwell on the description of lurid scenes, a certain kind of obsession, and so forth. That is, what is represented expresses the speaker; it makes his inner being accessible.

Thus to the fact of the possible interdependence of the functions already noted, we may now add that of their potential distribution, in a consecutive duplication of dimensions, on distinct but functionally superimposed planes.

As we see, an analysis of the phenomena of language reveals relationships that are more complex than those exhibited by Bühler's model. For example, representation (as the union of the sign and the image of the thing spoken about) can *function* appellatively. In other words, *the functions are not necessarily only effects of the perceptible sign proper* (as the model holds), but rather, and more frequently, effects of a larger unit that, to some extent, already includes all the perceptible sign's semantic dimensions. In fact, whatever acts appellatively already includes in some way both what is represented and what is expressed (as well as an appellative action of another order). This larger operational unit cannot be called a sign except in a special terminological sense, a sense similar in one aspect to Saussure's concept of sign, which, as is well known, denotes the unit formed by *signifiant* (a general image of the perceptible sign, or "sign" in the ordinary sense) and *signifié* (a concept). Here, as regards the unit of actual speech, we could very well speak of "symbol," without stretching common usage (and this designation would in part coincide with Kainz's terminology). "Symbol" would then be the term for a unit of speech having *immanent, internal semantic dimensions,* and not (as in the nominalistic manner of Bühler's terminology) for the pure perceptible sign taken in its relation to the thing spoken about.

In his model Bühler conceives of the semantic dimensions as so many (external) relations between the perceptible sign and the apexes of the communicative conglomerate. Taken in the usual sense, the names "symptom" and "signal" fit this conception in a way that "symbol" does not. The triplet signal-symbol-symptom, then, confuses two different levels: the external and the internal semantic dimensions of speech. Bühler has intuitively based his schema on the phenomenon of a concrete speech-situation, but has taken into account only its apexes, the termini of the relations: the perceptible sign, the states of the speaker, the things mentioned, and the listener's reaction. On such a basis it is incongruous to speak of "symbol" and "representation," and no less so to generalize about the entirety of language. Bertrand Russell clearly saw the external relations of the sign as precisely that, and his terminology is accordingly correct. He asserts that "Language serves three purposes: (1) to *indicate* facts, (2) to *express* the state of the speaker, (3) to *alter* the state of the hearer."[17]

In Bühler's model a genuine vision of the linguistic phenomenon resulted in an inexact conceptualization, with a consequential confusion and concealment of semantic orders. But this conceptualization can be corrected. His model must be refashioned, with special attention being given to its limits and terminology, as a schema of the concrete language-situation seen from the viewpoint of its apexes. Moreover, there is the added task of specifying the internal dimensions of the sign or symbol as a unit of speech—that is, its intrinsic structure. The unjustified pretension to totality on the part of Bühler's model (evident in its terminology), entails an unexplained negation of the sphere of ideality inherent in all signs and all speech. Thus a kind of inner replica of the external semantic dimensions—in a different realm of things—remains invisible. Yet it is present, of necessity, in every communicative situation, in all language. This will be shown by a description and analysis of the communicative situation.

10. *A Phenomenology of the Concrete Communicative Situation*

Description

Let us imagine a situation involving language in which one person says to another: "That bird is flying in circles" or, an even simpler example, "That animal is white." Let us further imagine that the animal in question is visible to both speaker and listener—that is, an element in the field of vision in which this communication takes place. This way we have a language-situation in which the three apexes (speaker, listener, and object) are perceptibly present. The form of the situation is simple and homogeneous. This avoids ambiguities and permits a more succinct description of the essentials.

The spoken sentence is a constitutive part of an action by the speaker. The sentence characterizes the action as communicative, and the communicative action, in turn, characterizes the existing situation as communicative. The speaker's action is directed to his listener and relates to an object in their common field of vision. The spoken sentence is both product and medium of the communicative action.

An action of this kind has as its aim the influencing of another person; it is an instrument with which to shape another's state. The fact that this is a *communicative* action means that the action of shaping the other is primarily and fundamentally one of making the listener share some experience, of making speaker and listener both party to a certain state of consciousness or, more simply, to a certain consciousness. This communicated consciousness is consciousness of a situation. By virtue of the sentence in question a new situation arises that is shared equally by both parties.

To act communicatively on someone means to place him, through the agency of sentences, in a certain situation.

The determining elements of this *communicated situation* are: the object, included by virtue of the communicative action that made it intentionally present; the speaker's attitude, made manifest through his action; and the action itself, the transitivity of which (a producing of the other's perception) establishes the common ground. Contained within this communicated situation (as part of the speaker's attitude, made manifest by his action) there is the expectation of a corresponding attitude of response—inasmuch as without it a communicative action (always of necessity intentional) is inconceivable. This expectation of a reaction, inherent in the meaning of a communicative action, reflects the essentially appellative character of this action. Communicative action is in essence a call or appeal.[18] The appellative dimension of the sentence is the attribute imposed on it by the fact of being part of a communicative action.

The *communicative situation* includes, in addition to the *communicated situation,* the completion of the communication: the reception and acceptance of the communication—that is, of the communicated situation, by the listener. In this acceptance (from which a listener can withdraw voluntarily or involuntarily, and in which case, through refusal or incomprehension, the communication fails of completion) lies the foundation of the responsive attitude.[19]

As we see, the appellative and expressive dimensions of the sentence are, strictly speaking, *values that inhere in the entire communicated situation,* even if they clearly have the sentence as their base. (It is, of course, the produced sentence, through the completion of the communicative action, that makes possible the constitution of the communicated situation.)

We have now described the communicative situation without express reference to the sign, or to its semantic functions or dimensions. We said that the medium (and, at the same time, the product) of the communicative action, was the sentence. An analysis of its vehicular (*medial*) function will provide us with observations regarding the nature and structure of language itself.

The sentence, as sign, makes manifest, in the manner of a symptom or index (we could also say signal, or indication, using the latter word in a sense that is conventional, but opposed to Russell's aforementioned usage), the ever-complex attitude of the speaker, and, as the salient part of this attitudinal complex, the attitude that makes the speaker just that, a *speaker,* someone who speaks, who addresses himself or herself to the listener in a communicative action. The manifestation of this fundamental part of what is made manifest is necessarily prior to all other manifestations of the sign, since without its perception it would be impossible to perceive particular meaning-intentions, which are comprehensible and apprehensible only as intentions of someone bent on signifying, of someone wanting to say something. This first function of the sign can be explained as follows: the sentence, as perceptible element of the communicative action, is an index of this action and, through it, of the agent as agent. In the sentence, in a certain way, we perceive the speaker as such—that is, as communicative subjectivity, in the inadequate (external) manner that Husserl spoke of (even though he refers only to the perception of acts that give meaning, but whose perception, I believe, is based on the more elementary one I am referring to). The sentence as sentence is indicative of the speaker as speaker. When I apprehend the speech as a speech, I apprehend the speaker as speaker, because the speech as speech is both indicium and perceptible part of the communicative action. But at the same time I apprehend myself as spoken to; I perceive the appellation that is operative as essence of the communicative action *qua* interhuman action: the action is aimed at me, and it can reach completion only if I accept the initial situation it entails—that of acting on me, of placing me in a new situation. Primarily, this appellation is simply a demand that I *comprehend* the sentence-meaning, receive it as wholly a sentence, and accept the speaker as speaker: a demand that I become interlocutor and listener.[20]

Expression and appellation, in their most general forms, are the first moments of communication, and immediate dimensions of the sign as such, inherent in the recognition of the sign as a sign. These functions of the sign are thus the basis for its allusive or referential power. Having once recognized the sign as sign, the speaker as speaker, and myself as spoken to, I can proceed to intuit the acts of reference (which I presuppose are inherent in every linguistic sign), and to recognize the mention of the object. In its turn, this activation of the semantic dimension in the direction of the object precipitates new expressive and appellative moments that are no longer general but singular in character: over and above his condition or attitude as speaker, the reference to a white animal manifests the speaker of our example as a subject interested in particular circumstances, as capable of particular observations, as desirous of some attitude on the listener's part regarding this particular object, etc.; the appellation, over and above the demand made of the listener to be a listener, becomes focused on the circumstances of the communicated situation; the reaction demanded, a result of the acceptance of the proferred situation, is one related to the communicated situation. In this way the dimensions of the sign become vehicles for one another, in a structure of superimposed planes. In projecting them, our intuition constructs the global meaning of the sentence, and with it the communicative situation, replete with its highly complex semantic dimensions. This uniquely rich action displays the being of the speaker with incomparable expressiveness.

This part of the discussion already shows what relative good sense it makes to schematize the sign's functions according to the apexes of the concrete communicative situation. The sentence as sign, as perceptible structure, is, in the final analysis, what makes the state of the speaker perceptible, what renders the object of reference intentional and shared, and what effects a reaction in the listener. The perceptible sentence is the fundamental instrument of the phenomenon of verbal communication.

When the sign is considered in this way, as medium and product of the concrete communicative action—that is, as an individual entity, *hic et nunc*—we can say that it *acts* on the listener, demanding his attention for the object at which it points, so that later he may assume an attitude toward the situation determined and presided over by the designated object. Moreover, because it is an instrument that is the product of a communicative action (addressed to the listener, determined by the object), the sign is a *symptom* of the state of the speaker or communicative agent.

Consequently, the functions of the sign in a concrete communicative situation can be summarized as follows: (1) to make the speaker's state perceptible, as product-symptom of the speaker's state (manifestation or expression), (2) to act appellatively on the listener, in its capacity as vehicle of communicative action (appellation), (3) as intentional mention, as description, reference, or naming, to identify the object that will determine the communicative situation (identification, or "indication," in Russell's term). We may therefore call the sign in these three semantic dimensions, respectively, "symptom," "signal," and "identifying indicator."

The specific phenomena of the expression of *affectivity*, and of the so-called "stylistic devices" of the language, which are usually studied in unjustifiable isolation in most theories of language, should be seen in connection with the schema we have outlined, integrated into the broad areas of the manifestation of the state and character of the speaker and of appellation. The phenomenon studied in Bally's stylistics must be understood as the presence within the system of signs of the language (*langue*), along with the denominative forms, of other forms whose purpose it is to enrich and intensify the manifestation of the speaker's inwardness and his effect on his listener.

Analysis: The Ideality Underlying the Concrete Communicative Situation

The preceding description focused on the effective, situational existence of the linguistic sign, with special attention being given to its concrete and its outermost dimensions. This has made it necessary to neglect, or barely touch upon, the sign's ideal spheres, to which we alluded above. But an analysis of the communicative situation will uncover them as necessarily operative there. The functions of the sign in the concrete communicative situation have their necessary foundation in the sphere of immanent and general (ideal) signification.

Although the perceptible sign is a real individual entity, and the apexes of the communicative situation to which it is related are real individuals as well, the relations obtaining between them are not simply relations between individuals. A mere relation between individuals could never be a semantic or linguistic one. The sign itself (for example, the word "animal," spoken in our example-situation) in order to *be* a sign and *act* like one, must be *recognized* as a sign (or word), and, what is more, as exemplar of a class of signs or words, as the concretion of an ideal model (as it might be conceived, for example, phonologically). The word "animal," as a sign-element of the *langue,* is the class of all utterances that actualize its phonological pattern. In other words, a sign, in order to function as such, has to be recognized as the token of a type. This does not hold, of course, for the being and action of just any object. The recognition of the presence of the abstract configuration in the perceptible singular entity allows me to apprehend it as a certain linguistic sign. Because of this I perceive the speaker's action as intentional and communicative (and not, for example, as a cough or other natural occurrence). The linguistic sign does not act communicatively—that is, *qua* linguistic sign—simply as an event (for example, as the falling of a stone produces ripples in the water), or simply as a perceived event, for that matter. For it to act as a linguistic sign, it must be recognized in its generality, it must be apprehended as a sign. However, the sign in the concrete communicative situation must be and act first as an event causing perception, so that it would be incorrect to deduce from the preceding analysis that what acts communicatively is not the perceptible sign but the idea. Both are present in the communicative action.

On the next level the intervention of the ideal entities is even more evident. An exemplar of just any class of signs will not serve to allude to precisely *that* object. The function of the individual, perceptible sign "animal," of mentioning this individual, perceptible object in this concrete communicative situation, is made possible by realms of generality. We could not allude to this same object by saying "That stone is white," for example. And this holds not only for common nouns. Demonstrative signs like "this one," "that one," etc., include to no less an extent a sphere of generality: in the concrete communicative situation, *this one* is always an object present in the communicated situation. And so forth.[21]

The upper levels of the *manifestation* of the state of the speaker (those grounded in the object's mention), similarly demonstrate the operation of ideal entities. The sentence is a complex symptom of an individual state of the speaker by virtue of the fact that, on saying it, this speaker is perceived as someone who speaks *a sentence such as this*. In other words, a general characteristic of his linguistic act, a characteristic I recognize, is the medium for my apprehension of the speaker as someone who, in a situation like this, is capable of an action like this one, of references and perceptions like these (capable, for example, of making a casual observation in a serious situation). The attitude, state, character, and inner being of the speaker are accessible through the perception of these universals present in his communicative act.

The total appellative function of the sentence will depend, in turn, on my recognition of the general (ideal) characteristics of the communicated situation in which I have been placed.

What are the implications of this evidence that ideal entities are necessarily present in the experience of concrete communication? We have seen that the concrete sentence is only effectively a sentence by virtue of our recognizing the generalities of a sentence in it, and of a class of sentences, that is, by virtue of our apprehending the sounds *hic et nunc* as something that is, for example, *the* sentence "That animal is white" (the sentence *in specie*). In turn, its concrete meaning is made possible by the general meaning of the sentence "That animal is white." The general reference (what Husserl, in fact, calls the "meaning"—*Bedeutung*) is inherent in the sentence *in specie*, which is to say inherent in any concretization of this ideal configuration.[22] By virtue of being a sign (that is, of being perceived as such), the sign necessarily carries this ideal meaning within it. We are justified here in calling this meaning the immanent or inner meaning of the sign. In another sense, because this general meaning is one and the same in every situation in which the sentence in specie is used—that is, whenever it exists *hic et nunc*—it is legitimate to term this meaning "suprasituational."

What has been said of the indicative-identifying dimension holds equally for the other dimensions. The sentence carries an *immanent communicative situation* within it, precisely the one we spontaneously imagine when we comprehend an example-sentence like "That animal is white."

Since apprehension of the elicited spheres of generality is a prior condition for the concrete functions of the sign, we may assume that the former are to a degree independent of the latter. For example, it sometimes happens that the mention of an individual object falls short of completion: the object is not found where the mention indicated it would be. The uttered sentence, then, is wrong. This eventuality does not entirely annul the sign's indicative-identifying dimension; obviously, in this case, the sentence is not without any referential meaning; the sentence continues to aim at a specified object *inasmuch as the sentence already prefigures it.* A general image of the object is always inherent in a meaningful sentence, whatever the outcome, success or failure, of its circumstantial identifying indication. The sentence (the representative meaning of the sentence, more precisely) *imitates* the individual object by projecting it as generality, in its essentiality.

In such cases of "failed" indication, the inner signification becomes visible, like a ghost in broad daylight which has been unable to disappear into its real counterpart. When this is not the case, the inner meaning becomes transparent and disappears in its perfect correspondence (adequation) with the perceived object; in this way, according to Husserl, the meaning-intention disappears in meaning fulfillment.[23]

The *expressive* immanent semantic dimension can also achieve this same visibility and independence in the concrete communicative situation. Every real concrete sentence is necessarily one spoken by someone and is the manifestation of their inwardness *hic et nunc,* but an insincere sentence, for example, can exhibit the ghost of an expressed immanent and general inwardness that contrasts with the concrete inwardness that other symptoms reveal, and of which, on another level, the same sentence, by being insincere, is one indirect manifestation.

The paralogical consequences for Bühler's model of ignoring this immanent signification are obvious, especially (but not exclusively, as we have shown) in the sphere of the representative dimension. Within the model being criticized, a *false* sentence is inexplicable: since the state of affairs described by the false sentence does not exist (by definition or by analytic necessity), such a sentence, according to Bühler's model, ought to be entirely without any representative function and dimension; but if this were the case, it would be impossible to understand how we could ascertain *which* state of affairs, precisely by not existing, would establish the falseness of the sentence, and therefore how, in general, we can know when a sentence is false or how we can know, for that matter, about false sentences at all. (If, on the other hand, Bühler is taken to be saying that only the immanent state of affairs—that is, the inner representative meaning—is what is represented by the sign, then in terms of the model there would be no way of distinguishing false sentences from true ones.) The sense or immanent meaning of the sentence is a necessary condition for its being true or false. Bühler's model fails to distinguish between what is spoken about and what is said of it (between the indicated-identified and the immanent-represented). In other words, it does not distinguish the object of what is said from what is said of the object. If I say, "This door is old," what is it that is represented? Is it the door I speak of, in its entirety, or only the door's-being-old? Husserl cleared up this point with his distinction between *object* and *fulfilling* sense (see below, Appendix I). The distinction goes back to Frege's separation of sense (*Sinn*) and meaning (*Bedeutung*), and much farther back to the theory of language of the Stoics. In this regard, Eugenio Coseriu pointed out to me that Bühler's model does not entirely correspond to the Platonic determinations of speech to which it is expressly indebted. Plato should be understood as stating that language is an *organon,* in which *someone* says *something* to *someone else* about *something.* There are five elements here, not just four, and there is also the distinction between what is spoken about and what is said of it.

Similarly, in terms of the model there is no explaining either expressive insincerity (which presupposes a difference between the concrete inwardness of the speaker and the immanent and ideal inwardness of which the sign is the bearer), or failed appellation (which presupposes a difference between the concrete effect actually produced by the sign and its intrinsic ideal appellation).

An autonomous and independent unfolding of the inner semantic dimensions is impossible in the concrete communicative situation, in which, by definition, the ideal orders are subordinated to the real functions. Yet every real sentence belongs to a concrete communicative situation.[24] Is there any way, then, to make the immanent meanings autonomous, so as to display the inwardness of language? This raises the question of the possibility of the existence of unreal sentences. The purely imaginary and fictitious sentence is, as we will see, the medium of the autonomy of the ideal spheres of language.

11. *The Meaning of Speech as Situation and as Unit of Thought*

Our study of the communicative situation has demonstrated the complexity of the semantic dimensions of language, or of what, in a broad sense, we may call linguistic signification. This signification may seem to be, at first glance, a group of different objects and relations, with no more unity than their common situation. That contradicts our usual conception of signification, according to which the signification of a sentence is an intellectual whole, a single unit of meaning. Our ordinary conception of signification comes, to a large extent, from the use of dictionaries, and in point of fact refers not to the sign of speech, but to the sign of language (*langue*), and above all to the word as a unit of the system of the language. This explains, in part, the contradiction mentioned above, for the signification we have been studying is that of the sign of speech (*parole*). But there persists a resistance to accepting a view of linguistic signification which dissolves it into a plurality of elements in a situational conglomerate.

Nevertheless, this resistance is only partially justified, for what we have here is a matter of different perspectives. In truth, the communicative situation has been described, in the preceding pages, from an outside vantage point, and all its elements appear as autonomous entities that stand in close relation to one another. For the speaker and the listener, however, the situational aggregate is a totality of sense, which their perception unifies in a complex and homogeneous image. This perception of the communicative situation, which the interlocutors necessarily possess, is the signification of speech *as a unit of thought*.

It should also be pointed out that despite first impressions, there is no essential difference between the signification perceived by speaker and listener. Both necessarily perceive, more or less thoroughly, the entire communicative situation—except that each knows himself to be identical, in either case, with a different element of the situation; both know they are located differently within the situation they share. The speaker and the listener each perceive, and necessarily live through, the situation and the perspective of the other: to communicate is to be, in a certain sense, the other party.

The perception that any participant can have of an actual communicative situation is necessarily imperfect, however, because an uninhibited contemplation is incompatible with participation in a practical act of communication. In specific types of situations in which the listener's participation is decidedly passive-receptive, his perception can, of course, be less impaired than the speaker's. Is pure contemplation of the communicative situation, or a knowledge of it that is uncurtailed by participation, possible? Such knowledge is in fact possible when the object is a *purely imaginary* communicative situation. This is precisely the perspective of the reader of literature.

12. *The Model of the Communicative Situation as Semantic Structure of the Linguistic Sign*

We will now outline the successive moments in the construction of a communication. Communication is, to an extent, an objective structure, undertaken and, in the main, anticipated, and then in fact lived through by the speaker. The listener, in turn, undergoes the same structured process, knowing himself to be the addressee of its meaning. The particular succession of these moments here proposed is essentially designed for the sake of establishing not a real temporal order (its temporal succession is problematic), but rather the order of logical-structural priority (remember that this schema is the result of our *analysis* of the communicative situation). The analysis uncovered an order of ontic foundation, corresponding to a unitary simultaneity in immediate experience, where these structural moments are imperceptible or disappear.

The sequence of the whole communicative process is as follows: (1) An act of the speaker takes place that has as its result or product the sign as a perceptible fact or event; more concisely, the sign occurs and the listener perceives it as a physical fact. (2) The listener recognizes the sign (perceptible fact) as a sign. (3) The listener recognizes the producer of the sign as speaker (the first moment of the expressive function of the sign). (4) The listener recognizes himself as addressee of the sign (first moment of the appellative dimension of the sign). (5) The listener intuits the concrete meaning-intention of the speaker, his "sense-giving act" (Husserl), and then, intuiting in this event its generality or essence, he comprehends the intrinsic reference to the object—that is, the sign's immanent representative meaning (Husserl's "meaning," Frege's "sense"). (This is the first moment of the representative or indicative-identifying function.) (6) The listener perceives the speaker as someone who speaks of such things, of things of this kind (the expressive moment that derives from the intrinsic representation). (7) The listener comprehends the (intrinsic) general material sense of the appellation: he intuits what kind of attitude is expected of him. (8) The listener perceives what is intrinsically expressed (the type of speaker's attitude revealed, in general, by the spoken sentence—by a sentence such as this). (9) The listener comprehends the intrinsic appeal that derives from a general expression such as this one. (10) The listener perceives the independent intrinsic appeal proper, and with it he grasps the whole intrinsic appellation. (11) The listener comprehends the intrinsic expression deriving from the total intrinsic appellation, and with it he grasps the whole intrinsic expression. At this point the act of recognition of the sign as *this* specific sign, as an example of this particular class of sentences (for example, the sentence-type "That animal is white") ends. (12) The listener perceives the concrete indication of the object, he knows to what individual object the speaker refers; at this point the intentional signification (which is the immanent representation as actualized and aimed at an object) becomes filled with concrete meaning; the "sense" is "fulfilled." (This perception carries within it the perception of the concrete inwardness of the speaker as *intentional mention* (meaning-intention) aimed at the object—the first moment of number 5.) (13) The listener perceives (inadequately) the concrete inwardness of the speaker; he comprehends the whole expression. (This moment also implies, reciprocally, the moment just listed above, number 12, since only the perception of the mentioned object makes possible the characterization of the way the speaker mentions it, and this characterizes the speaker, reveals and expresses him.) (14) The listener perceives the concrete appellation, the concrete situation in which he has been placed. (He perceives what J. L. Austin called the "illocutionary force" of the speech act.) (15) The listener assumes the communication. That is, he becomes in deed the addressee of the appeal. (This act of the listener can be seen as the beginning of the "perlocutionary" effect of the speech act.)

We can diagram the physical sign-event, given in sensory perception, as a circle; and the sign as the object of an understanding that recognizes it as *a determinate sign* (and, therefore, *as a sign*), as a larger circle drawn outside the first one. The communication is structured around this center.

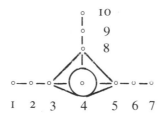

The numbered circles represent: (1) the perceptible speaker, (2) the concrete inwardness of this speaker as manifested in the communication, (3) the intrinsic expressivity of the sign, (4) the perceptible sign recognized as the sign that it is (as perceptible event plus the ideal configuration given in it), (5) the intrinsic appellation of the sign, (6) the concrete appellation of the communicative situation, (7) the perceptible addressee (listener), (8) the intrinsic representation, (9) the (concrete) fulfilling sense (the intended aspect of the object), and (10) the concrete object mentioned.

Once the sign is produced, this entire system exists as potential to the situation and as expectation on the interlocutors' part. The steps set forth above mark its effective realization in the experience of both listener and speaker.

Starting with the perception of the primary intrinsic dimensions and moving through the perception of the derived intrinsic dimensions (derived from the mutual determination of the primary ones) and on to the perception of the external or concrete primary dimensions (the act of mention, the object mentioned, the concrete action appealed for) and those derived from their mutual determinations (the more highly nuanced expressive and appellative dimensions)—the apprehension of the communicative situation (foreseen and intended in the main by the speaker and perceived by him and by the listener) consists in successive determinations of the parts, one by another, of the parts by the whole and of the whole once again by each part, until the final determination of the concrete communicated situation, of the communication as act, and of the total communicative situation is achieved.

This reciprocal determination of the whole and the parts can also be diagrammed, in a less detailed sketch than the former one, as a succession of structures, each one added to, and enclosing, the one before it.

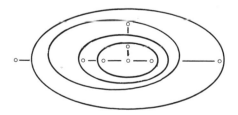

III. *Language and Literature*

The question whether there is an essential formal difference between literary-poetic and the other kinds of discourse, especially ordinary language, has never been resolved. On the one hand, not even the most rhetorical lover will speak in sonnets, and only the most unscrupulous journalist will report consistently in the manner of an omniscient narrator. Thus some forms of speech tend to be peculiar to literature: On the other hand, some great literature is written in a language that is not intrinsically distinguishable from ordinary discourse; and there is often "literary language" in texts lacking a strictly poetic design. I conclude that the difference is to be found in the fact that poetic language with all naturalness can—but does not need to—assume forms that, although perhaps possible, are aberrant and counterproductive in nonpoetic discourse. The foundation of this exclusive potentiality is the ontic nature of literary-poetic speech. Because poetic discourse is *fictitious,* it can be now similar to ordinary discourse, now entirely dissimilar from any real utterance. In other words, because poetic discourse is fantasy, it can be by turns fantastic or realistic. The distinctive potentialities of poetic discourse reside in the freedom of imagination.

In this chapter I present the phenomenon of fictive discourse and discuss its basic implications.

13. *Literary Language*

Real Authentic Sentences, Real Inauthentic Sentences, and Imaginary Authentic Sentences

A real authentic sentence is one that, as a perceptible product of a speaker's communicative action, effects communication by causing the listener (the addressee) to perceive and comprehend it as a communicative sign. The production and perception of the sentence determines the scope of the communicative situation, a scope that may be narrow, as sometimes in the case of a copresence of speaker and listener, or broad, spatially or temporally (written sentences, recorded ones, etc.).

A real authentic sentence may be present itself or be represented by a vicarious sentence. If I tell someone of a dialogue I have had with a third party and, in direct speech, say: "He said: 'Pedro is my friend,'" the sentence "Pedro is my friend" that *I* pronounce *hic et nunc* as part of my account is not a real authentic sentence but the representative of a real authentic sentence that was spoken by the third party in question. Of course, the sentence "Pedro is my friend," in my direct speech, here and now, is a sign. But it is not a *linguistic* sign. If it were, it would mean that Pedro is *my* friend, which, obviously, is the meaning neither of my account nor of this nonlinguistic sign. The nonlinguistic sign "Pedro is my friend," *signifies* (that is, refers to that of which it is a sign, "represents" it) in a way that is different from *linguis-*

tic signification: in its performance as a sign, the ideal entities of the immanent meaning of a linguistic sign play no part. This nonlinguistic sign *reproduces in fact* that of which it is a sign, it materially recreates it; the imitation, in this case, of what is being represented is not a semantic dimension but the very being of the sign. (If I understand Charles S. Peirce and Charles Morris correctly, this sign could be included under their conception of an "iconic sign," a concept Peirce created.)[1] The linguistic sign is both symbol and imitation solely by virtue of its immanent signification (see Appendix I I I). Between the (merely conventional) perceptible linguistic sign and the thing signified, there is always immanent signification (which is a mention *in specie* of the thing and is not merely conventional). But a sentence that is the representative of another token of the same sentence-type does not signify in this same way, and for this reason we can say, in this sense, that it is not a linguistic sign. As a sign it belongs to a different class from the strictly linguistic sign; it is, rather, of the same kind as the sign of the representational plastic arts, portrait painting, etc. (to the extent that these works are considered signs of the objects they represent). These reproductive sentences seem to be sentences, then, without this being the case. Therefore, we will designate them as pseudo-sentences.[2]

Now then, the capability that we have just identified, of speaking (or writing) sentences that are not sentences proper but representatives of (absent) authentic sentences is what makes possible the introduction of *merely imaginary sentences* into the realm of communication. In other words, we can pronounce pseudo-sentences that represent other, authentic, but unreal, sentences.[3]

The virtue of the pseudo-sentence is to make present an authentic sentence from *another* communicative situation (whether real or merely imaginary). To comprehend a sentence represented in this way (that is, to fully grasp its semantic dimensions) is to imagine its communicative situation, to imagine it in the context of its communicative situation. In the example just given, the situation to be imagined is determined by the explicit mention of speaker and listener. This localization or determination of the iconically represented sentence, when it is imagined in this way by the comprehending listener, guided by the context provided by his present communicative situation, corresponds to the original and normal use of pseudo-sentences—that is, the common manner of quotation.

Literature as Imaginary Language

In view of the above, the extraordinary thing is the existence of pseudo-sentences with no concrete context or situation—that is to say, of sentences iconically represented by pseudo-sentences but imagined without any external determination of their communicative situation. *Such is the phenomenon of literature.* The fundamental convention of literature as a human experience is to accept these sentences as language and to attribute meaning to them generally.

In properly reading a poem, we apprehend the graphic signs not as sentences (like the sentences we find in a letter, for example), but as pseudo-sentences, with no concrete context, which represent imaginary authentic sentences. The "situation" of every poem is, simply, the (historical) realm of the spirit; and its context none other than the implicit determination of its being a poem (at times made explicit in its title or presentation). Our reading a poem consists of the task of comprehending these imaginary sentences, which, as far as their (missing) situational predetermination goes, no one has ever said anywhere to anyone. To comprehend them, then, is to imagine their situation without any auxiliary determinations—that is, to unfold the situation immanent in the sentence, to project the situation imaginarily on the basis of its vehicle, the producer from the product, and the object from its description.

Every (absent) sentence that is represented (whether by

pseudo-sentences—that is, iconically—or by description in authentic sentences) has, as such, an imagined situation, but only the literary sentence has an imagined situation without accessory determinations. Literature is the pure development of the situation immanent to the sentence.

The concrete situation of *reading* literature may be defined as a concrete "language" situation, or communicative situation, in which there are only pseudo-sentences. Is this, properly speaking, a *communicative* situation? It is, but not a *linguistic* communicative situation. The reader is the addressee not of author's sentences but of pseudo-sentences. The imaginary authentic sentences that these pseudo-sentences represent are not, *qua* authentic sentences, sentences of the author, inasmuch as they are not perceptible products of his communicative action (a real person could scarcely pronounce imaginary sentences). The author communicates to us not a particular situation (a communicated situation) by means of real linguistic signs but, rather, imaginary linguistic signs by means of nonlinguistic ones. In other words, the author himself does not communicate with us *by means of* language; instead he *communicates language* to us.

The relation of the author to his work is, therefore, although comparable, different from the relationship of a speaker to his sentences. His works are not *linguistic symptoms* of the author, in the way that speech is of the speaker. In this sense, the work does not express the author. Of course, in another way it does express him, or make him manifest, just as a product, in general, expresses its maker. But between the author and the language of the work there is no immediate relation, as there *is* between a speaker and what he says.

Since what is communicated is (imaginary) language, the imaginary linguistic communicative situation—that is, the immanent signification of the sentences—includes neither the author nor the reader; it is a transcendent object for both. Linguistic appellation, expression, and representation-indication do not occur in literary communication, which, as we have shown, is not linguistic communication. But as imaginary functions of the communicated language, all three constitute an object of contemplation for the reader—and for the author as reader.

In ordinary speech there is an awareness of the semantic values immanent to the sign, and these are used for practical purposes—that is, they serve in a capacity subordinate to the concrete situation. If the use of these internal dimensions is highly self-conscious, we may designate such speech "rhetorical." On the other hand, no use of language, whether self-conscious or spontaneous, can properly be termed poetic. Language is the object in poetry, or poetry is language itself as object. This assertion, however, is ambiguous and inexact. We should say: there is no poetic use of discourse or speech. All discourse is use of the language (that is, of knowing the language and how to use it). Moreover, discourse is used practically and has functions (which we have studied). Now then, we can speak of a poetic use of the language (*langue*), but not of a poetic use of discourse (*parole*): for discourse itself, when imaginary, *is* the poetic use of language and is not itself then used poetically, as though poetry were a goal somewhere beyond discourse. Imaginary discourse is itself poetry. And poetry is not praxis, but theory, vision. One could say that poetry has theoretical functions, but this would be a tautology: it would be like saying that poetry is poetry. Of course, poetry may have, in addition and externally (not intrinsically), a practical function, ends that are not theoretical but appellative. Strictly speaking, the communication of poetry (declamation, publication, etc.) is a practical act.

It is incorrect, I think, to say that language has an aesthetic function, as though there were a fourth function, located on the same level with the three we have studied. One *can* say this, in another sense: language (as a human capacity) permits man to give shape to the stuff of inwardness—that is, it makes intuition possible—and so one can properly speak of a possible aesthetic function of language. But actual discourse has no aesthetic *function:* it is, when imaginary and the object of contemplation, *itself*

the aesthetic phenomenon. On the other hand, we cannot say that
real discourse in and of itself is its own practical effect, or the
concrete inwardness it expresses, or the object it indicates. Such
external relations of the linguistic symbol are truly functions, and
correspond to needs whose satisfaction the sentence was designed
to serve.

The above observations contradict Croce's view that poetry
and ordinary speech are essentially identical (along with artistic
intuition and ordinary intuition, or aesthetics and linguistics),
differing only quantitatively, in richness. The ordinary sentence,
I maintain, is real, the poetic sentence, imaginary. The ordinary
sentence belongs to a concrete situation, of which the speaker and
the listener are both a part; and this situation is the ultimate
meaning of the sentence. The imaginary sentence, by contrast,
immanently signifies its own communicative situation, and
neither the author nor the reader forms a part of it. Both author
and reader can, therefore, *contemplate* the situation signified
and, what amounts to the same thing, the sentence. The real
sentence and its semantic dimensions, on the other hand, cannot
be an object of contemplation for the speaker and listener. (They
can only contemplate, after the fact, an imaginary sentence that
is, to a greater or lesser extent, a replica of the real sentence
already in the past—that is, recall the situation.)

This may also explain the intellectual discomfort we experience when we hear expressions like ''In this novel the author tells
the reader . . .,'' ''With these words the poet expresses his feeling
that . . .'' (understanding that he does it directly and linguistically), ''The work is a dialogue between author and reader . . . ,''
''The literary work is the author's message'' (understanding it is
a direct, linguistic message), and so forth—modes of speech that,
taken literally, falsify the nature of literary communication.

The persistence of such phrases is due to an understandable
confusion into which appearances lead us: since literary creativity
tends naturally in this direction, undoubtedly the literary work
can be, and normally is, ''communication'' from author to

readers (but only in the sense of an object that is the content of a communicative act); and in a work we find, as its constitutive material, configurations that are linguistic in an obvious way; ergo (now comes the mistaken conclusion) the literary work is a linguistic communication, like any other. What is overlooked is that the vehicle of the communication is pseudolinguistic, and that the language of the work is not really communicative language but a communicated imaginary object.

The literary work is not the communication but what is communicated. The communication is a practical, material event. The literary work is an imaginary object. It makes ambiguous sense to say that poetry is (real) communication. Poetry is an imaginary object and, in consequence, a cognitive act (in which the imaginary object appears)—that is, intuition (nowadays misleadingly called "consumption," by some critics, by others "reception"). It is image and intuition. Poetry is image that has the form of language and the structure of a situation of linguistic communication, but it is neither real communication nor real language. It is quite another thing to say that this image may be, and mostly in fact is, communicated—this latter event being, as Croce has shown, a practical, not a theoretical, fact. Moreover, the distinction between imaginary authentic sentence, real authentic sentence, and real inauthentic sentence makes possible an adequate explanation (regarding poetry) of Croce's assertion that art is theory, and its material realization (as actual communication) a practical matter outside the realm of aesthetics. At the same time, it would be a misunderstanding to give these distinctions a *psychological* meaning, as though they were empirical determinations regarding the artist's creative processes. Intuition and "extrinsication" (Croce)—that is, the production of a material icon of the intuition—are not two stages in artistic creation, but two different and philosophically distinguishable levels of human activity, whose real temporal relationship (precedence, simultaneity, alternation) is not a philosophical but an empirico-psychological problem, about which it makes little sense to hazard groundless generalizations, and regarding which it would be inappropriate to attempt any a priori determinations.

The claim, current in the theory of literature since the assimilation of Ingarden's book, that the literary work is a configuration of language or of sentences (*Sprachwerk, Satzgefüge*, etc.)[4] acquires, with the preceding clarification, a precise meaning. The methodological postulate of many New Critics, that the author is not a part of his work nor the work a part of the author, that each is transcendent to the other, as Wellek and Warren insist (and Ingarden and Kayser before them), is strengthened by our demonstration that the author is no part of the communicative situation of the communicated imaginary sentences that make up the work. The author, a real being, is not and cannot be part of an imaginary situation. Author and work are separated by the abyss that separates the real from the imaginary.

Consequently, the author of works of narrative literature is not the narrator of these works; nor does lyric poetry consist of sentences the poet says. That is, the poet, as such, does not speak. His writing or his recitation is not a *linguistic* communicative action, but the production of pseudo-sentences.[5]

The speaker (lyric, narrative, etc.) of imaginary sentences is as imaginary an entity as the sentences—that is, an immanent dimension of their meaning, one element in their immanent communicative situation. The speaker of literary sentences is the *expressed* (or revealed) element in them; the addressee, the *appellative* element immanent in them; the object, the *represented* element immanent in them. Literary fiction, therefore, is not only the fiction of narrated events, but the fiction of a complete narrative or, in general, communicative situation. The being of the literary work is constituted not only by the fictive world of the work, long since recognized as such, nor by this world plus the fictional narrator, found by Kayser in studying the novel, nor even by both of these plus the fictional reader, which, as Kayser also indicated, belongs to the work[6]—but by all of these together with the *fictional sentences,* whose immanent meaning the other three elements are. (To use terms of recent French criticism: literature is the fiction of both the *sujets de l'énoncé* and the *situation de l'énonciation.*)

The Poetic Work as Real Communication in a Public or Historical Situation

In the light of what has been said in the preceding pages, the following point must be made: The whole literary work, as an object produced by the poet and contemplated by the reader, must be viewed as the content of a real (but nonlinguistic) communication of the author in a real communicative situation: the historical situation shared by both author and reader, an extended concrete situation that is by no means private in nature. This communication, or product, expresses the author (nonlinguistically) and has a (nonlinguistic) effect on the reader. In addition, it can perhaps be said that this communication refers to something, is a *sui generis* symbol of the world, an artistic symbol. On a plane distinct from the linguistic one, then, there are also relations of communication surrounding the poetic work. There is an artistic expression of the author, and there is an appeal to the contemplator and a representation of what "it" is. There is also, therefore, a degree of sincerity and depth in the expression, an intention of artistic effect, either successful or frustrated, and artistic truth or falsehood.

Empirical Author, Ideal Author, and Fictional Speaker

The author objectifies himself in his work as creative mind, and as such, as creative mind, he can be spoken of on the sole basis of the documentary evidence of his poetic creations; for the author as creative mind is nothing but what originates the work—one supreme moment of the author's concrete self—and not the real person in all his determinations. The objectified, ideal author is not, then, the speaker of poetic sentences (as basic speaker or as a character) nor the poet's empirical self. A new conceptualization of this matter was introduced by Wayne Booth in *The Rhetoric of Fiction*.[7] He distinguishes the "real author," the "implied author," and the "narrative voice." It seems to me that these terms correspond to our triad of empirical author, ideal author, and fictitious narrator.

14. *Linguistic and Literary Functions*

Karl Bühler makes passing reference[8] to the correspondence of the three functions of the linguistic sign to the fundamental modes or "functions"[9] of literature: expression would correspond to the lyric mode, appellation to rhetoric, and representation to the epic and dramatic modes. This suggestion, taken up and refined by F. Kainz, W. Kayser, and B. Snell without further development, deserves a disquisition of its own. In Snell's treatment, with his pairing of expression and lyric, appellation and drama, representation and epic, the correspondences receive a more adequate specification.

Every communicative act necessarily involves all three semantic dimensions, so that the imaginary sentence, too, must exhibit them all. The fundamental literary modes—lyric, epic, dramatic—will therefore, if indeed they do coincide in some way with the semantic functions, correspond to the *predominance* of (in each case a different) one of the dimensions over the other two.

The old notion of the lyric mode as subjective poetry takes on new life in this regard, once we bring to bear the new concepts of

87

the semantic dimensions that we have developed. In the first place, we can dispense with the conception of the subjectivity of the lyric mode as a thematic determination. That is, once we admit the correspondence of the lyric mode and the expressive semantic dimension, we can no longer consider the lyric subjective *because it is a speaking about the speaker* (since, on the contrary, it makes no difference what is spoken about there). The lyric mode would now be a predominance of the expressive dimension, of what is made manifest without being said, over that which is said and that which is appellatively induced. In other words: a poetic work would be in the lyric mode if its substantive part consisted of the fictional speaker as "expressed." If we conceive of the expressive dimension of language in the broad sense explained in Chapter II—that is, not restrictedly as the manifestation of "affect" or "affect and volition" (or "attitude"), but as the revelation of the speaker's being in the linguistic act, we would then discover, in the expressive dimension of the sentence and in lyric poetry, a special mode of communicating and objectifying by means of language, one whose power to reveal is peculiar to itself. This makes possible a conception of lyric poetry as the unfolding of the linguistic potential for making something manifest that is *not* said by means of something else that *is* said (or represented). Consequently, we can state—giving new meaning to the rhetorical topos of ineffability—that lyric poetry is the mode of communicating something that is in essence unsayable. This makes lyric poetry a fundamentally different revelation of being (with different possibilities) from the epic and from philosophy, which are essentially a *saying,* that is, a representative revelation, thematic speech.[10]

That peculiar insensibility to lyric poetry, that species of occasional incomprehension we describe as not "feeling" the poem even though its "logical meaning" (that is, its representative dimension) is clear to us, is more readily understandable with the aid of the foregoing distinctions. The hardest poems to feel are often brief sentences with the simplest of representative meanings, dealing with ordinary things and events. An ear deaf to lyric poetry signals a failure to perceive the expressive dimension, an incapacity to respond spontaneously to the overtones of what is being said.[11] To understand lyric poetry is to attune oneself to the tonalities of what is represented. Consequently, this understanding presupposes a logical understanding of what is represented.

One could conceive of a sign or a language in which the representation were merely an empty, gestural dimension, the sign being reduced, in this respect, to a blind or merely feigned act of pointing, with no indicative value, no conceptual or imaginary contents. Perhaps the language of music corresponds to the idea of "phrasing" or "discourse" in which subjectivity is mobilized, ordered, and objectified only in expression. This would make music the extreme form of the lyric mode or the greatest imaginable potentialization of expression.

The epic mode or narrative can be characterized by the predominance of the representative dimension of discourse. The substantive part of an epic work is the world constituted by the imaginational contents of the mimetic sentences, their representative meanings. The expressed speaker and the appealed-to listener are incomparably less apparent factors in the epic; at times mere empty forms, they are imperceptible.

Finally, the dramatic mode would be the one in which language is predominantly appellative, inasmuch as the sentences in drama are simply sentences of the agonists, instruments of dramatic interaction. A narrative or an expressive effusion, when spoken by the characters, is only dramatic if it functions appellatively in the sphere the characters inhabit, if it is subordinate to the action.

If we now recall our conclusion (above, Section 13) that the literary work, as contemplated object, is always a (complete) communicative situation, an unfolding of the immanent semantic dimensions of the imaginary sentence, we can improve upon the characterizations of the basic literary modes. The predominance of one or another of the semantic dimensions is only the foreground of the phenomenon: the literary modes are distinct basic types of imaginary communicative situations.

The idea, often suggested but never developed, that the literary modes represent or correspond to basic modes of human existence, to essential aspects of mankind (Ortega, Kayser, Staiger, and others, assert this without elaborating the pertinent theory), may well find its point of theoretical departure in this conception of the typical basic communicative situations.

Lyric would be the communicative situation of speaking to oneself, in solitude. In this situation, what is *said,* the representative dimension of language, cannot be the dominant sphere, since the listener is himself the speaker, and the fundamental meaning of the communication cannot be to make known to someone what he already knows (to reveal to oneself what one already knows).[12] Nor could the appellative dimension be dominant in such a situation. If I want to assume a certain state of mind or adopt an attitude, I can generally do so without having to (or having it make any sense for me to) put myself in a certain situation by means of a communicative action. For the situation itself is normally immediately accessible to me. I essentially speak to myself if I want to *express* my state of being and to modify it through its expression. A saying in solitude makes sense mainly as the resolution of inner tension, as an act of *attuning oneself* to a particular tonality (this is indeed akin to appellative action), or as the objectification (always more or less indirect) of a disturbing or incomprehensible state of mind. What is done through speech in this situation is a reordering of one's inner being through a coming to know one's own state, which, made manifest in the communicative act, becomes objectified. Lyric poetry is imaginary soliloquy.[13]

The epic situation is the *narrative* one: someone with time and leisure spins out a long discourse treating of past events about which an equally unoccupied audience desires information. The difference between this fundamental communicative situation and the lyric situation is obvious. In a general way most conceptions of the nature of the epic conform to this determination of the corresponding communicative situation. Thomas Mann, Wolfgang Kayser, and Emil Staiger[14] consider as essential to this genre both the *preterite* character of what is related, and the unhurried pace, so removed from present concerns, with which the story develops. In essence, this conception derives from Schiller (letter to Goethe dated April 21, 1797).

This generic narrative situation gives rise to two kinds of communicative situation and literary work: (a) *epic* in a strict sense: oral narrative directed to a large audience, to a people taken collectively; and (b) the *novel:* a written narrative addressed to a lone individual (an "idle reader"). Remember that the narrator, whether speaking or writing, is always fictional, and never the author.[15]

Finally, the situation for dramatic sentences is the communicative situation of practical interaction, equally typical and basic. (Drama, because it is *imaginary* action, makes possible something that real action never affords mankind: the contemplation of its pragmatic being. This is why this particular poetic species, as "theory," has ethical consequences; in a privileged way it allows for ideological criticism. Staiger[16] points out that drama is capable of destroying beliefs, of shattering the framework of the religious conceptions of a nation. This is possible because it permits us to adopt a contemplative attitude and to put an ironic distance between ourselves and the action, the customs, and the convictions that regulate conduct.) As a type of literature, drama is characterized, in contrast to the lyric and narrative modes, by its lack of a "basic speaker," and by the fact that in it all the speakers are on the same logical level. These dramatic speakers are people whose discourse is essentially pragmatic action, and not simply "informative," as in the case of the epic speaker, or "expressive" as in the case of the lyric speaker. We might add that the scenic performance is a partial materialization of the semantic display of the imaginary sentences that constitute the dramatic text. (This situational concept of the literary modes is the basis, I think, upon which a speech-acts theory of literary discourse should be built.)

Literature is a way man has of confronting, by means of the imaginary, basic possibilities of his existence: to learn of the past by means of narration (the epic), to act communicatively in the human community (the drama), and to feel himself being, intuit himself as inwardness (lyric poetry). The reader does not actually engage in these forms of life, but "plays" them, contemplatively.

15. *The Dimensions of Language and the Structure of Narrative*

Our study of the semantic dimensions of the linguistic sign has made it possible to deduce that the poetic work, as the pure unfolding of imaginary sentences, necessarily exhibits a structure of three spheres, corresponding to the three orders of signification. We must now relate this conception of the structure of the work to the one obtained phenomenologically from the aesthetic contemplation of narrative discourse (above, Chapter I). A totally coherent melding of both these views is clearly possible, and the result is a more complete theoretical picture of the structure of literary narrative.

The World

The world that results from the imaginational projection of the apophantic content of the mimetic sentences is fundamentally the sphere of imaginary representation. Of course, the speech of the characters also belongs to this phenomenal stratum, but does not itself constitute a representative meaning of the basic narrative sentences (except when the dialogue is narrated—that is, is in "indirect style"). In the case of direct dialogue, a new stratum of three spheres is superimposed on the basic one (but subordinate to it). Naturally, in these dialogue-sentences the appellative dimension predominates. The characters' sentences (and among them those of the narrator *as character,* if he is one) differ from those of the narrator as such, because the former potentially belong to predetermined (imaginary) situations—that is to say, to situations determined not solely by the meaning immanent in the sentence. For this reason, the intrinsic semantic dimensions of the characters' sentences (unless they *narrate,* which as we have shown, doubles the structure of the narrative work)[17] are not allowed to develop fully; they are subordinate to the concrete (imaginary) functions of the (imaginary) perceptible sign in the (imaginary) communicative situation. This constitutes another difference, in addition to that of logical order, between the singular apophansis of the character and that of the narrator.

The phenomenal stratum "world" potentially includes, then, more than just the realm of the representative semantic dimension, although the latter is its necessary and fundamental substance.

The Narrator

The narrator, a continually present phenomenal stratum in narrative discourse, is, substantially, the sphere of the *expressive* dimension. This stratum also includes as part of its fundamental substance the (imaginary) perceptible material body of the sentence. The perceptible sign is there, aesthetically, as part of the speaker's communicative action, as his voice and diction, the bearer of his rhythm, melody, and tone. Potentially, this stratum may be enriched with *representative meaning:* the narrator may speak about himself. Additionally, the non-mimetic apophantic content of the narrative discourse (his aphorisms and so forth) may form part of the substance of the narrator.

The Reader

Lastly, the appellative dimension requires that we settle the question of its location within the phenomenal structure of the literary narrative. In our initial description (Chapter I), we did not mention a third stratum—the fictional listener. In certain works the narrator speaks about the listener, addresses himself to him in explicit appeal, vocatively, or imperatively. In such cases the presence of this third stratum is abundantly clear. In the phenomenon of the *essential* structure of narration, however, it is not easy to perceive this stratum, and for this reason we omitted mention of it. Now the time has come to complete that description.

That this necessary presence of the fictional listener is tenuous, transparent, has its cause in the characteristic nature of the narrative mode. The imaginary communicative situation (not predetermined; without extrinsic location) in which the fictional narrator speaks at length to the fictional listener—in short, the narrative situation—is essentially alien to immediate practical exigencies. It is an essentially *contemplative* situation (even if never wholly a contemplative one—see below). What particular appeal, what effect, what influence is inherent in this communicative action—that is, necessary to all narration? Only a very general attitude is solicited of the listener: a contemplative attention, a theoretical disposition to cognize what is communicated, a certain deference to the speaker. The basic trait of this appeal is the "Know that . . ." recognized by Bertrand Russell as a tacit appellative meaning in even the most theoretical sentence, those farthest removed from practical life.[18] To this appellative meaning can be added that of demanding belief in the truth and sincerity of what is being said, an appeal that usually accompanies the speaker's sentences about himself and his circumstances and about his "idle reader"—the fictional listener.

As we said, in the narrative there may be sentences concerning the fictional listener. Representative meaning, then, makes the latter at times almost as determinate as a character. But his necessary substance is the immanent appellative dimension of the narrative sentences. In them an image of the listener is indirectly objectified. This image is a projection of what the listener is for the speaker, and of what the latter wishes the former to be.

A narration with a high appellative dimension is, of course, more likely to be found in a dramatic communicative situation.

The intrinsic semantic meanings or dimensions of the linguistic sign of the basic discourse cannot be considered a phenomenal-aesthetic stratum of the literary work, since none of the three is visible as *meaning* in aesthetic contemplation: instead, they are imaginally projected as world, speaker, and listener. Of course, the perceptible sign itself does not disappear in this way, but neither can it be considered an independent stratum in the aesthetic actualization of the work: as we said, it crystallizes around the speaker. Strictly speaking, it could be considered a substratum.

Naturally, what the narrator says in the imperative mode to the "idle reader" is never (as no sentence of the work ever is) something the author says to the real reader. It is a (predominantly appellative) moment of the imaginary linguistic communication, communicated to us nonlinguistically by the author, and one which we contemplate. This understanding of fictional sentences resolves, I think, the age-old paradox about the words of the literary author, developing Sir Philip Sidney's classic statement, "Now, for the poet, he nothing affirms and therefore never lieth" (*The Defense of Poesie*). As we have already seen, the author of "fictions" verbally neither lies nor tells the truth, for in that capacity he affirms nothing: he does not speak. The narrator's protestations of truthfulness (and the narrator *necessarily* under-

95

takes to describe the world—adequately, in *truth*), and in this respect his entire appellative action, are moments of the imaginary communicative situation that, like all such moments, merely determine the character of the latter as an object of contemplation. The incorrect view of the literary phenomenon apparent in sentences like "The author tells the reader . . ." etc. generates paradoxes and falsifies, at times unwittingly, the nature of literature, as when we hear that an author of fiction tries to convince the reader of the veracity of his narrative so as to intensify the power of poetic "illusion."[19] The reader of poetry—necessarily an enlightened reader, with a knowledge of conventions and artifices—is not moved by tricks to accept the play of fantasy. If he were taken in by a supposedly true account, his contemplation would be impaired; like the fictional listener, and in his place, he would then only contemplate the speaker and the narrated world and not the whole communicative situation—and even these only imperfectly, since his participation in that circumstance would disturb his contemplation with thoughts about the truth of what was said and the attitude he should adopt with respect to it. Similarly, the reader of, or the listener to, lyric poetry is able to inhabit unreservedly the poem's expressive dimension—that is, possess the words not just in their representative dimension or solely as imaginary listener, but also, and essentially, as speaker (the predominant dimension of lyric poetry)—because of the poem's imaginary existence, because it is not real discourse by the poet. The real reader comprehends and actualizes the poem as fiction. Otherwise, he would feel himself included as interlocutor, as confidant, etc., and would thereby find himself distanced from the expressed resonances; he could thus only intuit them in a defective way. (Children's literature proper uses specific devices in order to induce the immature listener to adopt and maintain a contemplative attitude regarding the narrated world: the events of the story are situated in a distant and uncertain place and time, so that even the remotest practical concern is excluded.)

16. *The Ontic and the Phenomenal Structure of the Literary Work of Art: Critical Remarks on Ingarden's Theory*

This is not the context to discuss Roman Ingarden's ontological view of the literary work of art, but some critical remarks must be made regarding the conception of the literary object's *structure* presented in his *Das literarische Kunstwerk* (1931) and reasserted in his *Vom Erkennen des literarischen Kunstwerkes* (1968).[20]

Ingarden treats the literary object as an entity of a peculiar ontic nature, neither real nor ideal, consisting of different strata and constructed upon a twofold basis of realities (mental acts, physical signs) and idealities (ideal concepts—*ideale Begriffe*). According to Ingarden, each stratum of the work has its own values and, in addition, a particular function in the constitution of the work as a whole—that is, a structural relationship with the other strata. The relationship of these strata is one not simply of juxtaposition but rather of intimate mutual determination. The lowest stratum is that of the sounds of language, capable of specific literary values and at the same time, in its capacity as sign, the determinant of the next stratum. The second stratum is that of the elementary and complex meanings of the linguistic signs. Structurally the fundamental one, this stratum determines the constitution of the objectivities (people, events, things) represented in the work. In other words, the meanings of the sentences of the work project "states of affairs" (imaginary, purely intentional), in which the objectivities are constituted or displayed. The sentence founds the imaginary object. Between the meanings

97

(second stratum) and these objectivities (fourth and final stratum) there is a stratum of "aspects" or "views" (*Ansichten*) which is the sum of the possible perceptible manifestations of represented objects, their possible faces or appearances. This stratum is virtual, and is actualized in the reading, so that the imaginary objects may achieve a measure of visibility or, more generally, of pseudoperceptual presence. The stratum of objects is the central one for the *aesthetic perception* of the work: this one is the object of our gaze, which sees through the other strata. The function of the stratum of objects is not like that of the other strata: instead, this stratum reveals the metaphysical qualities (tragic, sublime, grotesque, etc.) which it is one of the aims of art to produce. In addition, this stratum makes patent the *idea* of the work.

The essential insight of this theory of Ingarden's is, I think, the notion of superimposed planes, with the lower ones providing a structural and ontic foundation for the upper ones. Rather than a vision of the phenomenal structure of the imaginary-literary, Ingarden's theory is the analysis of an order, a system of complex elements, that is of necessity present in every realization of the work as aesthetic object (in every reading or, in general, every experience of it). The nature of his theory can best be indicated by saying (from the point of view of a phenomenological-psychological analysis of the process of the comprehension of a work) something like the following: in order to experience a literary work one must first perceive the stratum of the signs and sounds (for example, *hear* the first sentence); second, understand the separate meanings of the words and, then, the larger units of meaning in which the meanings of the words are joined together and made more precise. These units, in turn, give an aspectually determined access to the described and narrated objects and states of affairs (the objectivities). The objectivities, in their turn, may give rise to the final quasi-stratum: the metaphysical qualities, ideas, etc. Naturally, we should think of each reading as a succession of units of comprehension (sentences or, rather, "lexias," according to R. Barthes' *S/Z*),[21] each involving all the strata, so that the on-going experience of the literary work is a continual coming and going among the strata, from base to apex and back again. In this sense it can be said that all the strata are given simultaneously. Of course, that is not to deny the order of precedence and founding, which is ontic rather than temporal. The idea of an entity with multiple constitutive mediations seems to be, as I said, the basic insight of Ingarden's theory.

Yet the following fundamental objection seems to me to be valid and of a certain theoretical importance. The assertion that the literary work is built up in this way of strata implies that in the full experience of the work, one necessarily passes cognitively through all these strata. But in no way does this mean that the *aesthetic phenomenon as lived* in that experience has this same structure. Ingarden himself points out, as indicated above, that the reader's attention is centered on the stratum of objectivities (*Das literarische Kuntswerk,* par. 28): this shows that in reading, perception is not equally distributed among the four or five strata. In his later work he notes more than once that meanings become *transparent* for the reader. It is also true that Ingarden distinguishes between the literary work as an unchanging, objective, and abstract entity and its "concretizations" or realizations in the individual reading experience. The concretizations fill the gaps and the indeterminate aspects of the schematic being of the work. But he does not see that they also change its structure. The fundamental differences between the ontic prearrangement of elements and their lived aesthetic configuration are not considered by Ingarden. He asserts that the concretizations have the same structure of strata as the "work."

I have shown that, depending on the type of literature, the lower strata disappear from the intuitive field or remain in the background (blurred but nevertheless relevant). Thus what the aesthetical-phenomenal object (the object experienced in the straightforward enjoyment of literature) really *is* is a final reordering of the work's being, wherein this is newly structured, with the ontic structure studied by Ingarden serving as the fundament for the new one.

On reflection it is easy to see that an aesthetic reading of a literary work does *not* give us the work articulated in Ingarden's four or five abstract, superimposed planes. (For proof one has only to read a few sentences of any narrative and apply the *intentio obliqua* of self-observation. Semantic contents of words, for instance, will not be a part of the phenomenological inventory.) Furthermore, it is a necessary condition for aesthetic perception that the ontic fundament of the reading experience be by-passed, hidden, circumvented, in an illusion of immediately intuited life.

Now then, the subject of my own investigation has been ultimately the structure of the work *qua* aesthetic object, as the imaginary unit offered to the reader's or listener's perception—in short, as literary phenomenon. Together with the description of the general form of the aesthetic object, I have indicated how the structure of this imaginary entity is related to the previous ontic structure of the work.

I believe, then, that the forms and elements brought to light in Ingarden's analysis do constitute an essential part of the literary process, but that the normal reading experience flows in the opposite direction; it moves from the scattered multiplicity of linguistic elements and articulating forms—the ontic prerequisites of the work—toward their integration and disappearance in the vision of a concrete imaginary world. This vision is the aesthetic experience and the work's consummation: precisely what a long tradition has called the contemplation of the aesthetic object, and what philosophers such as Bergson and Croce call the intuition of the singular. But this *presence* of the singular imaginary object also has a universal structure: the structure of the literary work as aesthetic phenomenon. The analysis and description of this structure, as I said, has been the theme of this book and gives it its title.

If we now essay an analytical schema of the ontic structure of the literary work, in the manner of Ingarden (a complete view of the strata of which the work's being is built), we have to correct his schema in three fundamental respects: (1) Above the stratum of the real signs (pseudo-sentences), we would place that of the imaginary signs iconically represented by these real signs. (2) The stratum of meaning would offer three dimensions. Besides representative meaning (the only meaning considered by Ingarden), the ontic base of the work would include the expressive meaning and the appellative meaning. (3) The stratum of "objectivities" or objective entities would also be threefold, with the addition of *speaker* and *listener* to *world*.

We can now extract from our analysis an answer to the question about the relation between the ontic structure and the phenomenal-aesthetic structure of the literary work, of its progressive constitution and its complete final presence.

The projection of this phenomenal structure on the basis of the ontic foundation we have described (a projection that follows naturally) is explained when we consider the structure of transcendental forms that determine the experience of literature. In fact the basic convention of accepting as full of meaning pseudo-sentences that represent imaginary sentences with no predetermined situation makes possible the unfolding of the intrinsic semantic dimensions, which themselves become the sentences' situation—in other words, disappear by being imaginally projected as world, speaker, and listener. The pseudo-sentence, the action of granting fullness of meaning to imaginary sentences with no situation, and, finally, the phenomenon of the imaginal projection or "alienation" of meanings are all transcendental moments that determine the experience of literature, that turn the ontic edifice mentioned above into the aesthetic phenomenon whose structure we have described.

Now we may also raise the question whether the strata or parts we have spoken about exhaust the structure of the literary work. As Roman Ingarden's uncertainty on this point shows,[22] this is not an easy question to answer. Where, in fact, are we to locate those "metaphysical qualities" of which the Polish philosopher speaks? It seems incorrect to say simply that they belong to the narrated world, for at times they suffuse the entire work, fill up and enclose the imaginary communicative situation. Where are we to locate the *irony* that (as in works by Thomas Mann— *Doktor Faustus,* for example) is an essential part of the work and is not the narrator's ironic tone, but a total perspective, that distances and ironizes the narrator himself together with the whole imaginary communicative situation?

In developing his theory of tragedy, Aristotle based his vision of its structure on a pervading concern with its ultimate climate, the *tragic* temper. In his conception, the rest of the work's structure (the form and elements of the story, the nature of all the parts) is subordinate to the production of pity and fear, the tragic sentiments. Apparently, essential aesthetic dimensions like these should be considered phenomenal strata (or parts) of the work. But at this point we leave the field of the *linguistic* structure of the poetic work, the field that the philosophy of language can illuminate.

17. *Derivative Logical Structures of Fiction and Varieties of Fictional Speech-Situations and Worlds*

In Chapter I of this book I advanced the thesis that in the fundamental structure of fiction the singular apophantic sentences (what I termed the "mimetic" sentences) of the basic narrator are taken (by the reader who knows how to read fiction) as being necessarily and unrestrictedly true. "Unreliable narrators" cannot be used in an argument against this thesis if they are merely characters among others and not the basic teller of the tale, because secondary speakers, according to my concept, are not logically privileged unless they assume the function of the basic narrator. But what if they do assume that function, what if a narrator marked as unreliable is the one that commands most or all of the narrative discourse? It is a fact that there are such unreliable narrations in fictional literature.

Two questions are involved here. First, do unreliable fictional narratives have a logical structure at all? And if so, are these logical structures related to the one I described and, furthermore, as I maintained, are they derived from it as from a fundamental one? In the following pages I will argue that unreliable fictional narratives do have a logical structure, and that their logical structures are indeed modifications of the basic one I described.

An Example of "Unreliability"

An example of unreliable fictional narrative is afforded by the first sentences of Ken Kesey's *One Flew over the Cuckoo's Nest*. It will be agreed that the example is fairly typical and comparatively simple. We will disregard the question whether the initial structure—to be described—is maintained throughout the novel, and all similar concerns about the singularity of this work. We will suppose that the reader only knows, before starting to read, that it is a novel, and also suppose that he continues to read beyond the few sentences quoted here.

> They're out there.
> Black boys in white suits up before me to commit sex acts in the hall and get it mopped up before I can catch them.
> They're mopping when I come out the dorm, all three of them sulky and hating everything, the time of day, the place they're at here, the people they got to work around. When they hate like this, better if they don't see me. I creep along the wall quiet as dust in my canvas shoes, but they got special sensitive equipment detects my fear and they all look up, all three at once, eyes glittering out of the black faces like the hard glitter of radio tubes out of the back of an old radio.

"Here's the Chief. The *soo*-pah Chief, fellas. Ol' Chief
Broom. Here you go, Chief Broom. . . ."

The Situation of This Speech. Let me first make some general
remarks about this fictional discourse, based on the theory of the
nature of literature developed throughout my book. Then, I will
discuss the strictly logical questions.

As explained in Section 13, the purely imaginary discourse of
literature generates its equally imaginary situation of communication. We all accept that purely imaginary entities do not necessarily obey what we consider to be the laws of reality; in other
words, imagination does not have to be realistic, it can be fantastic. Everybody knows that persons, places, and events presented
in literature often escape the limits of real possibility. What is
never observed is that literary discourse and the speech-
circumstance it generates, precisely because they are also purely
imaginary, can also be, and often are, of a fantastic shape and
kind. As I have indicated in another place,[23] it is precisely in
modern *realistic* literature that we find the most unrealistic types
of discourse and of speech-situations. Our example, belonging to
a novel that, after a moment of initial hesitation, appears to the
reader as standard realistic fare and deploys a world assimilable
to our everyday experience, creates, from the beginning, a really
impossible speech situation. Discourse such as the one represented in the quoted paragraphs is not a written narration based on
memory. It is an immediate description of ongoing events. But
neither can it be thought of as being a written record nor as being
spoken aloud (the reported actions of the emitter exclude both
possibilities). But the third possibility, that it be taken as interior
monologue, is excluded by the nature of its content: this is information that one does not have to impart to oneself. Besides, the
style strongly suggests communication to a listener. And it is so
taken by the reader. Thus what the reader imagines is a purely
internal speech that nonetheless is audible to a vague listener (an
invisible listener to interior monologues who, together with this

silent audible speaker, belongs to the family of the well-known "invisible witness" of third-person behavioristic narrative; it is the family of phantoms that populate the speech situation of realistic fiction). This is, then, another of the typical, utterly fantastic speech-situations that frame modern and contemporary realistic literature. By contrast, the narrative situation of a chivalric romance, in approximating that of a chronicler, is comparatively realistic.

This discourse, because it is imagined as being both audible to someone and not uttered acoustically or otherwise, generates a listener that is very close to the emitter, a phantom confidant that we, as readers, will adopt as our primary posture of reception. Such is the basic *appellative* dimension of this discourse.

As for the constitution of the speaker's image, he already presents himself in his second sentence as being a part of the world he is describing. Many of his sentences will refer to himself, and thus *representative* meaning will issue to build his image. But many *expressive* moments will also contribute to the development of his presence, such as the emphasis on the hateful attitudes of the orderlies, the anacoluthon in the fifth sentence, the implications of some of his assertions for his view of the world, and many more.

Having said this much about the general character of this imaginary discourse and the kind of communicating participants it generates, we will consider more closely its referential dimension and its strictly logical aspects.

The Deviance from Complete Circumstantial Credibility: Contradictions of Singular Features and of Universal Implications. Since the text does not begin with quotation marks and there is no indication of anyone introducing this speaker, the character called Chief Broom will function as the basic narrator of the novel as long as the continuity of this discourse is maintained. According to my conception, the reader will normally grant unrestricted credence to his (Chief Broom's) narrative-descriptive statements. Indeed, the reader will begin by establishing as *facts* of this fictional corner of the world the states of affairs asserted by the basic speaker in his mimetic sentences. There absolutely are black boys in white suits out there, up before the silent speaker.

How can this rule of credence be broken? Obviously, if the basic narrator were to make contradictory assertions referring to one and the same individual circumstance, the imaginary effort of the reader to constitute the pertinent feature of the narrated world would collapse. Neither could he accept both assertions contradicting one another, nor is there a criterion for choosing one. The referential dimension of the questioned sentences would be suspended and attention would fall back on the speaker and his state of mind. This would be the case if after the second sentence in our example we were to find something like "Nobody is out there in the hall." But such is probably not the most common form of unreliable fictional narration. As in Kesey's novel, unreliability (or the suspension of the rule of absolute truth regarding the mimetic statements of the basic speaker) is often produced by contradictions of a more indirect kind: not of singular apophansis but of the universal implications of the narrative-descriptive sentences.

All singular judgments carry universal implications. The thetic projection of a mimetic sentence establishes not only a singular fact of the imagined world (for instance, that black boys in white suits are out there before the speaker), but at the same time, inevitably, a general axiom for that world (that there are black boys in it who can at least occasionally be dressed in white). By establishing that singular sentence as true, we implicitly know, among other things, that the world of this novel is not the same as, say, the world of the *Edda;* we inexplicitly know that this has to be a country where there is a black population, etc. If a fictional narrator were to tell us that the King's daughter kept a unicorn in her garden, one of the general implications would be that such creatures are materially possible in that world. Clearly, the kind of world that the narrative displays is defined by this sort of implication of the mimetic sentences. We could say, using one of the current senses of the word "style," that such implications ultimately determine the style of the work. Or, to avoid confusion with the linguistic notion of style, we could speak instead of the *principles of stylization of reality* in the work, or of *the region of imagination* actualized therein.[24]

Now, a single work may display *successively* different principles of stylization without eliciting the sense of contradiction or of unreliability of the narrator. This reliable discontinuity of vision is found, for example, in Cervantes' longer fiction, in other works of the Spanish Golden Age,[25] and, I assume, in other literatures and periods. Unreliability of the narrator does occur when a definite law of imagination is constituted in the work and *some* of the narrator's mimetic statements have universal implications that are aberrant in relation to that law. This is most strikingly the case when the law of the work is, precisely, verisimilitude or realism.

Contradictions Resolved: Partial Unreliability. Reading Kesey's text, we are transitorily confused, after the first sentences, because the universal implications of the narrator's mimetic statements (that we are taking as being simply true) do not define a recognizable kind of world. That young blacks in white suits mop the floor of a hall is a possible and even probable occurrence in the world of ordinary contemporary experience. That such persons commit sex acts before starting to clean the floor is possible, although improbable, in the same world. That such persons carry sensitive equipment to detect fear in passing individuals strikes the reader as utterly improbable or as plainly impossible in the same world, though perfectly acceptable, by contrast, in the world of a science fiction narrative. The reading of the mimetic statements of the narrator as simply true has thus produced a constitutionally ambiguous imaginary world. If none of the evoked world systems were to dominate, all mimetic sentences of the basic speaker would stand as tentatively and uncertainly true, and the imagined world would stand as an ambiguous and anomalous imagined reality. This is certainly a possibility of literature (although not actualized in our example), and one that rests on a thus modified logical structure of fiction. Later, we will refer again to this ambiguous structure.

In the novel of our example, the realistic system of contemporary experience establishes itself unequivocally as the pertinent rule for this game of imagination. At the very moment that this is accepted by the reader the text is read (partly reread) in a modified way: those mimetic sentences of the narrator that have universal implications inconsistent with that rule are taken to be false. The falsity here turns out to be grounded not in a lie, but in self-delusion and insanity. We are led to this interpretation of the logical conflict because the generalized implications of the false mimetic sentences can be correlated inside a recognizable pattern of madness (distorted perception, hypersensitivity, erratic assumptions, sexual obsession, misplaced fears, etc.). Also because some of the mimetic sentences of the narrator that fit the realistic rule and are consequently held to be true describe him as a person of aberrant behavior. (Let us remark, by the way, that the indicated recognizable pattern of madness is the ordinary reader's notion of insanity and may be no more than a popular misconception. If this pattern of madness were objectively wrong according to science, Kesey and the reader would still be right in their acceptance of it as true, if, as Aristotle taught, the poet has to prefer falsity that is generally held to be true, over truths generally believed to be false. Similarly, what we just called the realistic system of contemporary experience—one among the possible laws determining imaginary worlds—is certainly not a scientific construct, but rather the historically tinged life-horizon of common sense.)

Since the narrator's sentence stating that the cleaning personnel carry sensitive equipment to detect the patient's fear is not accepted as true, its singular apophantic content does not vanish to become a feature of the narrated world. In that hospital, as it is imagined by the reader, orderlies do not carry instruments to detect the patients' fear. The representative-indicative meaning of the sentence freezes and remains attached, so to speak, to its utterer, and becomes a feature of his frame of mind: his is a mind that believes such a state of affairs to be possible. The major import of the sentence then becomes *expressive* (I am using this word as well as the other semiotic terms consistently in the senses explained in Chapter II). The referential meaning is rejected, and instead of an objective feature of the narrated world, the unreliability of the narrator is (indirectly, symptomatically) brought to the fore by the sentence.

(One might object to the preceding analysis on the grounds that the conditions of sanity and insanity, as well as the attributes of truth and falsehood, polarized in the confrontation of captives and establishment, are reversed in the ultimate allegory of this novel. But clearly this (not unprecedented) symbolic reversal of attributes could not occur in the novel if the initial and basic objectivity were not the one I indicated. If we were to read the novel so as to have the narrator uttering a metaphoric truth every time that he voices what otherwise is the expression of a delusion, an essential point would be lost, and the narrating character would cease to be pathetic and moving and become an inflated rhetorician. I doubt that one could hold to such reading throughout the text. But if so, this would be a case not of unreliable narrative, but of the basic fictional logic.)

As we saw, when the general implications of the mimetic sentences of the basic narrator are inconsistent—that is, cannot be reconciled under one and the same principle of stylization—the constitution of the imaginary world is suspended or frustrated or otherwise positively implemented as uncertain and unstable. If this hesitation of the reader is to be resolved into a definite law of imagination providing a stable world, as happens for Kesey's novel, there must be another principle determining which of the possible laws is going to rule the game.

There are at least three ways, I conjecture, of determining the ruling principle (that is, the region of imagination) in a work that elicits conflicting implications: (1) A quantitative preponderance of mimetic sentences implying one and the same type of world would result in the sentences of a deviant implication appearing to be invalid. (2) A sufficient number, not necessarily a majority, of mimetic sentences carrying the elements of commonplace, everyday experience and implying a realistic rule would force this seemingly privileged rule on the reading. (3) A sufficient number of mimetic sentences carrying characteristic motifs of one and the same traditional region of imagination (for example, the pastoral or the chivalric world) would establish that regional law of possibility and probability in the imagined reality. The second principle can be understood as a special case of the third one. The first two of these principles are operative in Kesey's novel. (I do not know whether there are or are not examples of unreliable narratives for the nonrealistic alternatives of the third principle.)

If in a hypothetical work there is no rule of imagination whatsoever, or, in other words, if no principle divides what is possible from what is not possible in a given world, no unreliable narrator can be constructed on the basis of conflicting universal implications. The most incredible statements (incredible from the point of view of a realistic rule, which would not apply here) would simply contribute to the display of an utterly fantastic and chaotic objectivity. Unreliability, in such a case, could be based only on direct contradiction.

The case (hypothetical or real) of a work developing its world under a new, unprecedented rule of imagination, one that may only *at first appear* to be more or less chaotic, is different. I believe that many great works, even if they do not always strike us as innovative, perform this historical deed. We must learn to read such a work from the point of view of its possible world. Cervantes' *Don Quixote*, because of its singular discontinuity of style, can instantiate the class so defined. Whether it would be feasible to complicate such literary experiments by adding to the new rule an unreliable narrator (that is, one who occasionally deviates from that rule) seems highly doubtful. There are practical limits to human imagination which probably apply here, even if the theoretical possibility of such a daring work seems unobjectionable.

Limited and Unlimited Unreliability

The form of unreliable narration that we have been considering through our example is a form of *limited* unreliability (or of limited reliability), since the conflict of the implied principles of imagination is, in this case, decidable, and, consequently, a considerable and well defined part of the mimetic sentences of the narrator will be unequivocally taken as absolutely true. Just as with narratives of the basic type, reliable throughout, limitedly unreliable narratives project a solid, consistent, and defined world.

However, the modified logical structure of these narratives does create a phenomenal difference in the constitution of the narrative work as a whole. As we saw, the invalidated mimetic sentences of the basic narrator reverse their structural role and, instead of being metamorphosed into concrete aspects of the narrated world, direct our attention to the mind asserting them. The dominant dimension of their meaning ceases to be the representative one and becomes the expressive one. This, in turn, implies that the narrator does not remain at our side looking, as we do, on the narrated world, but moves into the focal plane of the imagination, becoming obtrusive, just as he does by uttering universal statements, and for the same reason: as readers we suspend the validity of his universal assertions, just as we suspend (and reject) the validity of those of his mimetic sentences which deviate from the rule of credibility established in the work. In so doing, we let these sentences lend presence to the subject holding them, instead of letting them vanish into facts of the imaginary world. Thus, while reliable narrators can remain inconspicuous (if they abstain from universal statements and from making singular qualifications that ostensibly connote a subjective judgment—such as "beautiful," "impressive," "repulsive," "charming" and the like—that is, if they are "objective" narrators), unreliable narrators are *eo ipso* noticeable subjectivities and, if they are not part of the narrated imaginary world (first-person narrators), they nonetheless will always be sensed as a character-like presence. (Serenus Zeitblom, the main narrator of Thomas Mann's *Doktor Faustus,* is mostly a third person narrator—that is, not a protagonist of the events he is telling—and he is a good example of limited unreliability and conspicuousness. His unreliability, however, is not of the same logical kind as in Kesey's novel, as we will see below.)

The modifications of logical structure, as we see, are correlative to specifications of the communicative situation which, according to the analyses of Section 13, constitutes the basic phenomenic structure of the literary work. One could design a spectrum of narrators running from the utmost transparency to the densest presence. The objective, reliable narrator is extremely but not entirely transparent, because narrative sentences held to be true will immediately split into alienated apophantic content and residual linguistic form, and in the linguistic form at least the shadow of the narrator's voice will remain, as indicated in Chapter I. The degree of presence of the narrator will increase with the number of his self-references, with the number of qualifications connoting subjectivity that he makes, with the number of his universal dicta and of his exclamations, and, generally, with the density of *expressive* moments in his discourse. The most opaque presence will be reached by a narrator who, in addition to profuse self-reference, sententiae, and outpouring subjectivity, is unreliable. Unreliability, then, when it is limited, as we have discussed it thus far, tips the scales of the communicative situation in favor of the speaker, but it erodes neither the distance between speaker and the world spoken of nor the solidity of that world.

But what of *unlimited* unreliability? Unlimited unreliability of the basic narrator means that none of his mimetic sentences can be held to be definitively true, and consequently that no singular feature of the narrated world can be imagined as solid fact. The stable image, then, when it is reached in a work of unlimited unreliability, can only be the sequence of speech acts of such a narrator and the subjectivity they objectify: the stream of consciousness, the discourse of a mind. The represented world appears in this case not as an independent reality vis-à-vis the speaker, but only as an uncertain and unstable reflection in a mind. The interior monologue of Joyce's Molly Bloom can serve here as an example. This interior discourse is not undifferentiated in relation to the pertinent world, since some of its assertions will seem to be remembrances, some of them descriptions of actual perceptions, and some, expressions of purely imagined or dreamed events. But the privilege that we may accord to the statements in Molly Bloom's discourse that have the character of records of actual perceptions will be due not to a logical privilege pertaining to the game of literature, but to the general epistemological privilege that perception has over remembrance, imagination, and dream. Thus we grant a different kind of certitude to the things she is speaking of when they seem grounded in immediate perception (for example, Bloom lying at her side), in vivid recent memory (as her encounter with her lover), or in remote, already stylized memory (the premarital courtship). These discriminations are the ones we perform in ordinary life and belong to common-sense epistemology, not to the specific literary rules of reading.[26]

Is there no rule of a literary nature for reading such a text? Certainly, there is a fundamental one, which constitutes the return, on another level, of the rule of the absolute truth of the basic speaker's mimetic sentences. It is the rule that leads us to grant absolute certainty to the (imaginary) fact that this is, and is exactly, the interior monologue of Molly Bloom—a certainty that is of such an obvious literary and fictitious kind that it indeed lacks any real possibility. Thus the logical privilege applies in this case to the tacit statements of a latent basic narrator—the one who inexplicitly states "Molly Bloom thought: . . ." This form of total unreliability (meaning of logically unprivileged discourse) corresponds, then, to the general case discussed in Chapter I of the discourse of the characters who have not assumed the mimetic role of the basic narrator.

The unreliability of assertions made in interior monologues, as well as the unreliability of characters' speeches and of ordinary unprivileged speech in general, is unlimited in the sense of affecting *all* assertions of such a discourse. They could all be false, or all true, as well as some true and some false. But this is not the kind of unreliability that leads to plain rejection of the statements—as is the limited unreliability we discussed before. Characters' speeches, as long as they do not contain contradictory universal implications and are not directly self-contradictory, do receive some credence and display a (tentative, adjustable) world. But it is a world felt as dependent and relative, bound in substance to the speaking subject. It is seen as *his* fallible image of events.

The strongest unreliability is created when contradiction (either at the level of the mimetic statements or at the level of the principles implied) is persistent and undecidable.

If singular determinations of the narrated world are asserted and then denied, or followed by others that are unreconcilable with the first ones, the narrated world then assumes an uncertain presence, and the narrating or describing consciousness becomes both conspicuous and considerably opaque. This is the kind of inconsistency that distinguishes the narrators and worlds of Robbe-Grillet's novels. The opacity of the medium thus produced (an opacity to the second degree) converts the novel into a set of precise (discontinuous and unadjustable) subjective pictures of uncertain events. Nonetheless (or rather because of the occurrence of mimetic contradictions and of what I assume is a will for stable principles of construction), the law of imagination implied by the mimetic sentences in Robbe-Grillet's novels seems to be extremely consistent, mostly close to a realistic axiomatics.

The second kind of strongest unreliability of the narrator is the one created by a persistent and undecidable conflict of the implied laws of imagination. The world so projected does not solidify and is forever ambiguous. Juan Rulfo's *Pedro Páramo,* where the world of the living and the world of the dead indissolubly merge, exemplifies this development of contemporary fiction.

Varieties of Unreliable Fictional Speakers: The Logical Structures of Narratives

Not all kinds of unreliable narrators infringe and modify the basic logical structure of fiction. We saw that interior-monologue narratives and, more generally, narrations by a character have the logical properties ascribed by the fundamental norm to the speech of the characters, just as long as they do not assume the structural role of the basic narrator. Their unreliability is the normal unreliability of unprivileged discourse.

Also, *ironized* basic narrators, narrators characterized through their own discourse as being wrong-minded, can be constructed under the unmodified, fundamental logical rule of fiction. Serenus Zeitblom in *Doktor Faustus* or Lázaro in *El Lazarillo de Tormes* are characterized by their own discourse as somewhat unreliable. Zeitblom appears naive and limited by traditional ideology, and this derives from the parts of his discourse that relate to matters of judgment and conviction (universal statements, subjective qualifications, etc.). The reader not merely suspends but tends to deny the presumed validity of the maxims of Zeitblom's discourse; ironic distance is thus produced. Lázaro presents himself through mimetic sentences as a person of dubious upbringing and uncertain morality, and is not a narrator the reader would tend to identify with. But in both cases their *mimetic* sentences are unrestrictedly taken to be true. Their unreliability as persons, then, does not compromise their structural reliability as basic narrators.

It is perhaps unnecessary to remark that today we are acquainted with works of fiction that are not built of one continuous discourse, but rather constituted by a collection of discourses not subordinated to one another: the discourses of multiple narrating characters (as in some of Faulkner's works), juxtaposed heterogeneous texts (as in parts of Dos Passos' or Döblin's novels), and the like. These works or the pertinent sections thereof do not alter the basic logic of fiction; they simply use only a part of it (the unprivileged level of the secondary emitters) and elliptically suspend the basic narrator, who becomes a verbally inoperative potentiality—that is, who remains a permanent possibility. The central and ordering fictional consciousness does not manifest itself, in those cases, through direct speech (as it does when embodied in a basic narrator) but only as the presumed tacit collector and composer of the sequence of discourses or texts. The final metamorphosis of the basic narrator, and his logical privilege, is at work in this supposed act of selection and disposition of the icons of the words of others—that will be unrestrictedly accepted as representing the words of others. Thus some kind of fictive all-encompassing communicative situation will also be imaginally attached to literary texts of this form.

The expression "unreliable narrator" covers, as we see, several different phenomena, different kinds of fictional images that are constructed according to different specifications of a basic logical structure. First, there are unreliable basic narrators whose mimetic sentences are uncertain but are not necessarily false: dramatized and opaque subjectivities that we readers focus on, speaking characters whose discourse is the basic one of the work but does not entirely assume the structural function of the basic narrative and is deprived of its logical privilege. Their speech is sometimes unassertive and not distinctly narrative in kind; it is not always designed to picture a world vis-à-vis the speaker but often, rather, to register the flow of impressions and animic movements of which it is a part. Such discourses display the *reduced* logical structure; they lack the privileged level of apophansis. Molly Bloom's monologue can be taken as an example of this kind.

Second, there are unreliable narrators that speak *some* false and mostly true mimetic sentences. This is the derivative logical structure that emerges when the basic structure is complemented with an additional principle: the principle of world-consistency. We may consider world-consistency as a latent law of all literary readings, but it only becomes activated and noticeable when it is shaken. In this case, the awakening of the world-consistency principle responds to the conflict of universal implications of the basic mimetic sentences. Kesey's novel has been our example for this form.

Finally, there are unreliable narrators whose mimetic sentences of necessity cannot all be taken as true, but the reader cannot decide which are true and which false. This is the logical structure of unsurmountable contradiction, either at the level of singular determinations (exemplified by the self-contradictory discourse of Robbe-Grillet's novels) or at the level of their universal implications (the inconsistency of implied world exemplified by Rulfo's novel).

This cursory examination of alternative logical structures of fiction may strengthen the thesis that the logical structure described in Chapter I is indeed not only the traditional and today still the standard form of literary narrative, but also the generatively basic one. It is by restriction of that form through additional principles of validity or through structural ellipsis that the alternative forms constitute themselves. The fundamental "suspension of disbelief" of the fictional game is already selective (and thus Coleridge's formula cannot apply without qualification): it is limited to only one kind of assertion (the mimetic sentence) of only one kind of speaker (the functionally basic one). An additional principle, consistency of universal implications or of style of imagination (which applies in the case of a partial deviance of the universal implications of mimetic sentences from the dominant law of the imagined world) determines a limited suspension of the primary limited suspension of disbelief—that is, a selective disbelief *inside* the sphere of mimetic statements. In turn, *shortened* actualizations of the operating structure, which restrict the form to the one level of the unprivileged discourses of the characters (that is, exclude any basic narrator's discourse) displace logical privilege and certainty of image to the representation of verbalized consciousness or of objectified speech. And insurmountable contradiction (either in universal implications or in singular determinations) frustrates, negates, and suspends (but therefore still uses) the basic logic of fiction.

To suggest a possible Hegelian approach to this formal as well as historical matter, I want to indicate that there seems to be a dialectical movement of logical forms of narrative. Each of these structures appears to derive by way of negation from the (formally and in part historically) previous one. Also the basic logical structure of fiction can be considered derivative and as emerging, through negation, from real ordinary narrative, since the narrations of presumed fact that we hear or read every day are limited throughout in credibility, and we project from them an unstable objectivity. In real life, speakers are primarily fallible and never absolutely accurate and truthful. A speech intimating unrestricted truth of singular detail is in reality extremely atypical. In literature the primary teller is the one who never errs on a point of singular circumstances; the derivative and atypical basic narrator is the one who becomes, in this respect, unreliable.

Two final remarks. The use by the author of transitory deceptions of the reader is based on the logical structures we have described. Balzac's "leurres," pointed out by Roland Barthes in *S/Z*, would not be possible if the mimetic statements of the basic narrator were not taken to be simply true. Indeed, such deceptions constitute an abuse of the rules of the game. (They may obey another set of principles—not of logic, but of manipulative ethics or pragmatics.) Another form of transitory deception based on the fundamental logic of fiction is the use of characters' false statements that are not immediately but only belatedly declared false by the basic narrator. (This, by the way, is the reverse of *dramatic irony:* the characters, and the basic narrator, know something to be false that the reader, although restrictedly, because it is a character's statement, assumes to be true.)

Just as there is a reduction or ellipsis of the basic narrative structure, there is also a kind of overextension of the logical privilege. Reading some works (pastoral novels, for example), we feel that not only the basic narrator but also the characters speak the unrestricted truth (in the double sense of being sincere and of describing the fact to perfection), even when they are not assuming the function of the basic narrator. What could be called the principle of angelicality (since each character becomes a mouthpiece of the godlike narrator) pervades such works, flattening the logical differentiations of the image of speech.

Thus our provisional table of narrative logics contains the following forms: (1) unprivileged ordinary real narration; (2) fundamental, literary, fictional narrative (with privileged basic mimetic speech); (3) fictional narrative with overextended privilege (a privilege for all mimetic and even all non-mimetic assertions); (4) fictional narrative with restricted privilege (limited unreliability of the mimetic sentences of the basic narrator); (5) unprivileged fictional narrative (a tale told by a character who does not assume the basic fictional narrator's structural role); (6) unlimited unreliability in reference to singular circumstances (persistently contradictory mimetic statements); and (7) unlimited unreliability of the induced types of world (plural and contradictory systems of reality that are simultaneously implied).

Appendixes

I. *The Phenomenon of Alienation of the Mimetic Content of Narrative Sentences*

It is instructive to inquire whether the phenomenon of the alienation of the (singular) apophantic content of mimetic sentences could be described in terms of Husserl's theory of discourse. Can a theoretical account of it be given within the framework of his conception of meaning?

Traditionally, the immanent meaning of a sentence has been termed its "contents." The singular apophantic content is, in terms of Chapter II of this book, simply the intrinsic representative dimension of the singular sentence and, in Husserl's terminology, precisely the "meaning" or "signification" of a singular sentence.

We will first give a brief account of Husserl's theory of meaning, and then, from within his perspective, explain the phenomenon of the alienation of mimetic content. Because of its brevity, this presentation of Husserl's view is of necessity markedly interpretative; it does not pretend to be a paraphrase of the pertinent texts. Nevertheless, the basic terminology of the account is strictly his. It does not always correspond to the terminology used in the present study.[1]

The Basic Concepts of Husserl's Theory of Meaning

In his investigation entitled "Expression and Meaning" ("First Investigation" of the *Logical Investigations*), Husserl presents new arguments for the theoretical admission of the existence of immanent meanings. They are thereby seen as real and ideal moments of the communicative process. Basically, Husserl distinguishes the following moments in all communicative expression: (1) mere sensible "expression" (*Ausdruck*, the sign or mere expression), (2) "meaning" (*Bedeutung*, with respect to which the sign is a "meaningful sign" or an "expression" proper), (3) "manifestation" of inwardness (*Kundgabe*, with regard to which the sign is an "index"), and (4) the "object" meant or referred to (*Gegenstand*, for which the sign is a "name"). According to Husserl, between the meaning and the object of mention one must also distinguish (5) a "fulfilling meaning" or "fulfilling sense" (*erfüllender Sinn*), understood as the content of the perception of, or the imagining of, the object named, to the extent that this content is not simply the object but its aspectual projection in the conceptual form in which it is mentioned by the meaning.

The meaning, then, is not the object that the expressions name or its perceived or imagined image; the "naming" (*Nennung*, an identifying indication of the object) takes place *by means of* the meaning, and the perceptive or imaginal intuition of the object as object of mention (as intentional object), takes place only as predetermined and shaped by the meaning, which in each case is the particular conceptual form of the mention.

According to Husserl, meaning is the speaker's meaning-intention (*Bedeutungsintention*), the act that gives meaning to the expression *(bedeutungsverleihender Akt),* considered *in specie* or in essence. For example, the speaker makes the expression "The three perpendiculars of a triangle intersect in a point" meaningful with his *act* of so judging, by judging that, in fact, the three perpendiculars of a triangle intersect at a point.[2] The meaning of this expression is *not* that the speaker judges that the three perpendiculars of a triangle intersect in a point, but, obviously, that the three perpendiculars of a triangle do intersect in a point. And this meaning is not the concrete act of the speaker, but rather something that any other speaker can say, and in so saying say *the same thing.* Meaning, then, is the same something that is present in all the meaning-acts of the same class (in every actualization of the same sentence). It is precisely what distinguishes them as examples of the same class of acts of meaning (what distinguishes various renderings of the same sentence as being, not only phonologically but also semantically, the *same sentence).* Meaning is the species of the singular act of meaning: not the concrete act as such, but the ideal unit this embodies as the individual embodies its species, the virtual entity that is actualized in the act (of meaning); not the concrete judging, but the judgment as objective entity.

Evidently, not only the meaning, this ideal entity, but the real mental act, the concrete, individual, *hic et nunc* meaning-act as well, is somehow communicated by the sign. A sentence someone speaks communicates its meaning, but at the same time it externalizes the meaning-act of the speaker. This externalizing of concrete inwardness effected by the sign, simultaneous with its other functions, is what Husserl termed "manifestation" (*Kundgabe*). The meaning-act is not *all* that is made manifest, but the essential, nuclear part of it. (In addition, the perceptions or other acts on which the meaning-act is based are also made manifest.)

Just as it is possible, within this conception, to state that a meaning is the corresponding meaning-act *in specie* (Husserl expressly says this), it is also appropriate to say that the core of what is manifested (the meaning-act) is the concrete meaning, the meaning taken in its *hic et nunc* realization. There is, therefore, a certain coincidence of the meaning and the nucleus of the manifest; the latter is *concretely* what the former is *in specie*. Consequently, it is legitimate to speak, in terms of Husserl's conception (and this is thereby considerably clarified), of meaning as a *real and ideal* moment of communication, even if, for Husserl, meaning, strictly speaking, is only the *ideal* entity communicated. This explains why Husserl uses the terms "sense," "meaning," "meaning-intention," and "intentional meaning" synonymously.

Truth and Meaning-Fulfillment

Not every expression can be said to effectively *name,* and thereby accomplish a fulfillment of its meaning, since it is by no means necessary a priori that there be an adequation of the intended meaning, the object at which it aims, and the latter's possibilities of satisfying a conceptual solicitation. In other words, the judgment-meaning may be false.[3] Yet such a failure of the naming function and of the meaning-fulfillment does not render a particular expression meaningless; on the contrary, a meaning-intention is inherent in the very notion of falsehood.

When an expression (a word, a sentence) actually achieves "fulfilling meaning" and "names" an object, it is then "functioning cognitively" (in *Erkenntnisfunktion*). In this case expressions are, in fact, aimed at objects that they name or describe, in such a way that the perception or imagination (pure representation) of the object "fulfills' (*erfüllt*) or satisfies the meaning-intention.[4] It is in connection with this function that Husserl makes the aforementioned distinction between the intentional meaning (or signification, or meaning-intention) and the fulfilling meaning or fulfilling sense, which (unlike the intentional meaning or meaning *tout court,* inherent in every expression as such) is external to the expression, something that comes to meet it, proceeding from the named object, like the image a mirror gives back, to the intention before it. The fulfilling sense, if it really occurs (as we saw, this need not take place), will be an image that is symmetrical in structure with the meaning. In intentionally prefiguring the contents[5] of the perception or imagination, the meaning produces or elicits the fulfilling sense. One could say that we can see only what we try to see—and we see it *in fact* if our attempt falls within what the object will allow—that is, if the object is visible within our conceptual frame. ("Try" and "attempt" are words not properly used here, since "intention," in this phenomenological tradition, is preeminently a notion from the realm of knowledge, not of will.)

There is a fulfilling sense, the satisfaction of the intention in terms of which we address ourselves to the object, when the expression "functions cognitively"—that is, when the judgment constituting the meaning is true. Husserl's distinctions make possible a clarified view of the phenomenon of truth as adequation (correspondence of *intellectus,* meaning-intention, and *res,* object). Adequation is seen, then, as something that occurs in the upsurge of fulfilling meaning, in the object's satisfaction of the intention (whether in perception or imagination).

The Disappearance of Meaning

Husserl shows, in his analysis of meaning-giving acts (which, as we saw, when considered *in specie* are the meanings) and of the acts that fully satisfy the former acts' intentions (*in specie.*

the fulfilling meanings), that the adequation of meaning to object occurs as the *lived fusion of meaning and fulfillment,* a unity of "completion." In this union the two contents (intentional and fulfilling) "so overlap that in the living-through of this unity of adequation (*Deckungseinheit*), the object that is both *intended* (meant) and "given" is not double, but as *one* for us" (par. 14). And, later (par. 15, 4):

> Since, in the union of "completion," the intentional act is covered by the fulfilling act and so becomes fused with it in the most intimate way (if any grounds at all remain to distinguish them), it can easily seem as though the expression had only then and there acquired its meaning, as though this originated with the fulfilling act itself. This is the source of the tendency to imagine that the *fulfilling intuitions* are the meanings (in such cases the acts that categorically shape the fulfilling intuitions are overlooked).

With these sentences Husserl wants to demonstrate that meaning is something apart from the images that usually accompany our understanding of an expression; and to this end he points out that, in fact, in the lived-through unity of "completion," meaning and fulfilling intuition become confused, or, rather, the former disappears into the latter.

In the case of the literary work, this disappearance, I submit, is nothing other than the alienation of meaning in an image, of the mimetic sentence in an imaginary world (that is, the phenomenon indicated in Chapter I of this book).

It is suggestive to observe that it is almost closer to Husserl's notion to say that the fulfilling sense imitates the meaning, instead of saying that the meaning is mimetic and imitates the object. Nevertheless, the meaning can be considered the mimesis of the world, since an intended sense of adequation is inherent in its very being, and since the world is the *object*—rather than just its categorially predetermined or elicited fulfilling projection.

Ingarden,[6] too (as indicated in Chapter III), examines this phenomenon of invisibility or "transparency," which is an attribute of meaning when it "functions cognitively." In his view, the "sentence" or "meaning-content of the sentence" (the meaning of the apophantic sentence) projects, as part of the signifying intention, a "purely intentional state of affairs" or "purely intentional correlate." The projection "outward" of this correlate (the result of the affirmation of the judgment as true) in the direction of what has autonomous existence, brings about, in cases where the judgment is in fact adequate, the "identification" of the "purely intentional state of affairs" and the objective state of affairs. In this identification, the disappearance of the former takes place, and with it, one may add, the disappearance as well of meaning as phenomenon. Ingarden's work, however, does not contain sufficient development of these processes, or of their effect in the constitution of the literary object.

Threefold Alienation

The alienation of the immanent meaning in an image is not limited to the indicative-representational meaning that constitutes the singular apophantic content. All three of the intrinsic dimensions of the linguistic sign (and this is a phenomenal field neither Husserl nor Ingarden touch) are alienated in "image" in the literary work. The intrinsic expressed becomes the fictional speaker, and the intrinsic appellated becomes the fictional listener. But the alienation of these expressive and appellative dimensions is less noticeable than that of the representative dimension. This is because the felt or subjective distance separating the word from the thing indicated by it is great, whereas the distance between word and its (fictional) speaker is small or nil. Also, since the words are directed to the (fictional) listener and, in an obvious sense, reach him or her, the intrinsic appellated does not need to make a spectacular leap to achieve alienation.

The apophantic content that is not singular (as we saw in Chapter I) does not alienate itself: images are always (and only) images of individuals; it is therefore a priori impossible that there be imaginary intuitions adequate to general meanings and, consequently, capable of absorbing them.[7] General meanings ("thought" or "ideas") remain just that in poetic works. The same is true for words as structures of sound. Their inclusion in the narrator's stratum (cf. Chapter I) is due not to the phenomenon of alienation but to ordinary understanding, which links them to the producing subject who is their origin.

II. *A Transcendental Aesthetic and Logic of the Literary Experience*

Conditions That Make Possible the Production of Images

The mechanism of the alienation of the singular apophantic content in literature functions to perfection. Since, according to a basic law of literary understanding, the narrator's (mimetic or singularizing) discourse is simply *true,* the accomplishment of a fulfilling meaning is necessarily presupposed. In addition, since, according to another basic norm of the literary "game," the referential object does not exist but is a fiction,[1] any possibility of a *perceptual* fulfillment is discounted. That is, only an imaginary fulfillment is possible. Thus the production of images (we are not here concerned with what kind) occurs under optimum conditions, as if automatically: their sole determinant is the meaning, the mimetic content (no concrete memory or percept has any part). The adequation of meaning and "object," and their unity in completion or fulfillment, is, then, necessary (necessary in a literary reading), as is the invisibility of the meanings.

Here meaning, then, not only determines the form of *possible* fulfillment (as in the mention of a real object), but is adequate a priori, and possesses imaginary fulfillment, by virtue of the basic literary conventions involved. In fiction the meaning-intention is there only to be alienated. The rigorous functioning of this mechanism of imagination allows us to comprehend why the stratum of meanings is not a phenomenon in the literary work (that is, why it is not visible to a subject in the aesthetic attitude).

The consideration of these processes permits a more exact view of the literary phenomenon, of the constitution of the poetic object, and of poetic experience according to its fundamental norms. Aesthetic experience is generally characterized by an enjoyment of the image in and for itself, irrespective of any possible immediate theoretical-practical application of the contemplated image to the world. (This is the "nontranscendency" that, according to Ortega y Gasset, is an essential determinant of art.)[2] The most propitious mode of being for such an experience is the imaginary-fictitious. The merely imaginary is an object whose existence and characteristics depend on human will, and it has the practical-immediate nontranscendency of the unreal—although subsequently and on another level it may acquire a symbolic value with real appellative entailments. Literature is an imaginary object, of limitless possibilities, and the principal source of its constitution is the production of fulfilling images. This production is also a part of the comprehension of nonliterary narrative and descriptive discourse. In order to enable, assure, and enhance the production of these valuable images, readers willingly submit to precise laws regarding attitude and mental activity. So as to free the image from the practical context that would inhibit the exclusive enjoyment of it, the fictional image is selected, an unreal object, with no practical entailments. To assure the production of fulfilling images, in spite of the awareness of the unreality of what is referred to, the absolute truthfulness of the fictional speaker as to individual events is allowed within a parenthesis of irony. This is the way an imaginary object appears, and how poetic experience is produced.

Why we are pleased to enjoy these images, the meaning and function of this enjoyment in our lives, or what kinds of transcendence supersede this basic nontranscendency are all questions of a different order, like the question why some images are expressive and others are not. What concerns us here is the nature and structure of the literary object, the conditions of its possibility, and the basic constitution of the poetic experience.

Ingarden's Conception of Literary Sentences

Literary sentences are authentic but imaginary judgments, and not real quasi-judgments, as Roman Ingarden holds. He does not apprehend the merely imaginary nature of literary sentences. In addition to a failure to distinguish the different logical levels which we noted in Chapter I, his characterization of the apophansis of the poetic work is ambivalent.[3] According to him, literary sentences are "quasi-judgments." This indicates they are in a sense judgments but not seriously meant, which would be a reflection of the fictional nature of the objects at which they aim. If, however, as Ingarden believes, the truth of these judgments were restricted or "nonserious" *at the very level of the actualization of the sentences by the reader,* there would be no certain fulfillment or alienation, or, therefore, any plenitude of the literary object. But no such reservations attend the "serious" affirmation of the judgments that are part of a literary work, because the judgments in question are themselves imaginary, which is precisely what renders possible an unrestricted assumption of their truth. The lack of seriousness occurs on another level, as a *consciousness of play* that *enfolds* the mechanism that is productive of images. Poetic judgments (fictional apophansis) are judgments and are seriously meant, but they are imaginary, and the reader intuitively knows this.

The Natural World-View as Transcendental Form of the Poetic Experience

The several observations we have made in outlining a transcendental definition of the experience of poetry, the description of the structure of the *intention* of the reader of poetry and of his comprehension of the object as poetic,[4] must all be organized around two fundamental concepts: the understanding of poetic discourse as real and effective discourse, and the understanding of the world in which it is immersed as *our* world.[5]

What is implied in these two concepts is that the understanding of poetic discourse constitutes it in the beginning with all the attributes of real discourse, and that the understanding of the poetic world constitutes it, in the beginning too, with all the attributes of the real world. In this way the imaginary beings and objects of the literary work are *thought* of, from the beginning, according to the structures with which we ordinarily conceive of real objects: real objects are independent entities, susceptible of infinite determinations; offered to the knowing subject in (always partial) aspects; situated in continuous, homogeneous, irreversible time, etc., and in homogeneous, limitless space, etc.; are subject to causality; and so forth. And because they are purely imaginary, poetic objects *possess* this structure of reality as a formal characteristic. This formal nature is the foundation for the progressive constitution of their concrete characteristics, and their given aspects, in the unfolding of descriptive-narrative sentences, and according to the latter's particular content. (Of course, the content of poetic discourse may itself modify this initial formal nature of the poetic world, as happens in the case of "fantastic literature.")

In one sense it can be said that these two central concepts, which define the comprehension-constitution of poetry, unite in the concept of the understanding of poetic language as human language, as discourse in a certain language. For a linguistic community's natural world-view inheres in the everyday meanings of the words of its language. Thus, for example, if we read that Rocinante was a skinny nag, we think of him and imagine him, formally, from the outset, as a being with all the general attributes of his species, even though only his skinniness is initially an explicit attribute, an actualized aspect, given in mention. The other—the generic—attributes remain implicit, while the particularized ones are made to appear. Thus the implicit universe is an essential part of the literary work. And part of this implicit universe is the autonomy or selfhood of the fictitious objects. The concrete aspects that this world acquires through mention in the sentences of the work are projected against this formal horizon.[6]

There are transcendental structures that derive from the more fundamental ones. Thus, for example, the absolute truth of the singular sentences of the basic narrator leads to our spontaneously conceiving of these sentences, whenever they refer to perceptible events, as direct products of the immediate perception of the events they mention (since only this source could fully guarantee their validity). This, in turn, results in the speaker being thought of as *present* in the narrated event; and here we have the origin of his occasional status as "invisible witness" (which emerges whenever circumstances not including the speaker are narrated in that manner) as well as of that lack of temporal distance with which the events are offered. In such cases this lack of distance deprives the preterite tense of its usual temporal value.[7]

The Logical Content of Poetic Discourse and the Intuition of the Poem; Alienation as a Subsequent Act of Imagination

Even if we allow that the ordinary, immanent meanings of words in a language (such as "man," "day," "poem") are intuitions of an object, we must recognize that they are intuitions of general objects, universals, or essences, not intuitions of concrete singular entities, or images in a strict sense. For this reason it is natural to think of these meanings as concepts.

Since the words of the language constitute discourse, the latter contains concepts or general meanings, and, obviously, the comprehension of discourse as a meaningful unit presupposes understanding of the meanings of the words of the language that are actualized there. Thus the knowledge of the mentioned objects that we get from discourse is "discursive" (as opposed to "intuitive"), in the sense that discourse is a manner of communicating that conceptually grasps what it represents. Consequently, the individual-concrete object of discourse, it seems, cannot be intuited through discourse but only described by it. In what sense, then, is it correct to say that poetry is intuition, immediate knowledge of the individual-concrete? Since it seems certain that concepts mediate in poetic cognition, how are we to understand Croce's assertion that there may be no hint of a conceptual element in the words of a lyric poem?[8]

Poetic discourse, like all discourse, has a logical content. Ingarden's theory particularly emphasizes the basic role of ideal concepts and general meanings in the constitution of the poetic work. However, there is still the evident fact that our knowledge of poetry and of the objects mentioned in it is *not* an indirect knowledge by description or reference. The objects are there "in person" during our reading and in memory, unmediatedly, in their concrete-individual being. (Our knowledge of them is "by acquaintance," and not merely "by description," to use Bertrand Russell's terms.)

What happens is that all conceptual reference disappears in the act of reading, displaced by a direct vision of the objects, namely images. A subsequent, imaginative activity, then, overtakes the initial logical-intellectual comprehension of the discourse. This process, or what we have called the "alienation of apophantic content," can thus be understood as a succession of two mental acts: the first, an intuition of concepts or generalities that describe an individual, and the second, an imaginary intuition of the described individual, monitored by the prestructure of the description—that is, ordered by the (previous) conceptual mention. The literary stratum of objectivities is therefore a product of intuition guided by the dictates of the stratum of meanings.

In Henri Bergson's conception, poetry (as well as metaphysics) is an intuitive surpassing of the limits of language, itself the vehicle of concepts. Here the role of language is to lead us to a point from which the intuition of the object becomes possible; in other words, its role is to suggest, not describe. Through a suggested intuition the conceptual limits are left behind. Without necessarily accepting the whole of Bergson's conception, we can say that his is clearly an adequate view (in general terms) of the poetic phenomenon, as this has appeared in our study. To be more precise, we can say that it is adequate to the phenomenon of the whole comprehension of the description of an individual. Bergson's view seems in part to explain Croce's assertion. In all likelihood, what Croce had in mind was this second stage—poetic intuition—in which general meanings seem transmuted into an image of an individual.

In *Ideas on the Novel,* Ortega y Gasset remarks that concepts place us at a distance from the lived image of the object, and he asks the novelist not to *define* his characters, but to make them visible, to *present* them directly. As we have seen, the problem here is that it is impossible to present things directly in literature—that is, by means of language. Instead, there is, in the case considered by Ortega, the choice between two quite different referential modes: one, a summary or "telling" mode (Ortega's "definition") and the other, a minutely descriptive "showing" mode (Ortega's "dilatory mode"). In both cases, however, concepts are involved from the outset. In qualifying Ortega's thesis, we can say that the concepts in descriptive-dilatory texts are more susceptible of alienation than those in summary-definitional discourses.

III. *Toward a Concept of the Linguistic Symbol*

A Source of the Nominalist View of the Linguistic Symbol

Bühler's model suggests a nominalist conception of language, just as the model of behaviorism does. His schema of the concrete situation of real speech reduced the communicative constellation to the sign (the perceptible structure) and the concrete outer termini of the situation (speaker, listener, things). Even though Bühler's terminology of "symbol" and "representation" incongruously retains connotations of the inner or ideal dimensions of language, his model hides the phenomenon of thought. Obviously, in a communicative situation, the outer termini of the relation are the dominant presences and occupy the phenomenal foreground; on the other hand, the immanent meanings are not apparent but occluded, having vanished into the entities to which, in their different ways, they refer. Only in imaginary situations do the immanent meanings make their presence felt, but then, as we indicated, they are alienated in imaginary entities.

What originates the view of the communicative situation that Bühler's model, and nominalism in general, reflects, then, is the phenomenon of the identification or confusion of meaning and image (or fulfilling intuition), which results in the disappearance of the meaning and its alienation in the image. In words I quoted above (Appendix I), Husserl presents essentially this evidence.

The Meaning as Symbol and Imitation

One may well doubt whether we can speak of the *phenomenon* of thought, of meaning (as something different from perceptual or imaginary images). Our main argument thus far in this regard has been the theoretical point that unless we acknowledge the existence of such entities, the processes involved are incomprehensible—as Husserl shows in his "First Investigation." Nevertheless, the immanent meanings may be thought of as different modes of *imitation,* of reproduction of what they are a symptom for, of what they indicate, and of what they appeal to. What else but a *sui generis* imitation could meaning-intention be, and how else, if not through similarity, could it be related to its object?

As regards the relationship to what it signifies, the perceptible sign may be thought of as purely conventional. Its intentionality is "borrowed" (as both Husserl and Ingarden say), a product of the act that gives it meaning. At first—it is commonly thought—this act is arbitrary with respect to the choice of the perceptible sign's particular configuration. Convention then generalizes this borrowed intentionality, and the sign becomes a unit of the language. But our intuitive notion of meaning and its relationship with the meant object does not tolerate this view of the matter. How else, then, if not because of mere convention, could *this* particular act of meaning refer to *that* particular object? If neither convention nor a natural belonging obtains, it seems reasonable to conjecture that in each case *similarity* alone establishes the link between mention and object mentioned, symbol and object symbolized, between allusion and the object alluded to. (In structuralist terms: the link of meaning and object is metaphorical, while the link of perceptible sign and meaning is metonymical.)

Meaning is a ghost of an imitation, something whose nature can be visualized (mentally) with the help of the metaphor "incorporeal presence." (This figurative description helps convey the fact that although we can entertain concepts—that is, intuit them, or know them directly—we can have no images of them. Our intuitions of them are, in a sense, empty.) Meaning is, then, we could say, a *symbol* of the object. (More than convention is necessary in order to have a symbol. Saussure also makes this point: the link uniting symbol and the thing symbolized is "natural." This view of the nature of the symbol is based on the traditional meaning of this word, one that underlies common usage. According to this usage, it is improper to term the mere perceptible sign in its indicative function a "symbol." But this is not the case, I think, with the unity of the perceptible sign and its meaning—since the meaning is a symbol—on the level of both language [*langue*] and speech [*parole*]. The symbol represents the object symbolized. A nonsymbolic sign simply aims at it, by means of an established relation of contiguity.)

Of course, the symbol's mode of imitation need not be strictly iconic—that is, a reproduction of the configuration of the thing imitated. It suffices if there is some kind of similarity to establish the identifying relationship: for example, a similar impressive effect, a similar function vis-à-vis other elements, etc. (In the following section on the "symbolism of sounds" we will mention examples of noniconic imitation.) But it is also admissible that the configuration too is in some measure an object of imitation by the linguistic symbol. (Dámaso Alonso, appropriately, I think, insists on the "sensory" and "fantastical" components in linguistic signification.)[1]

The symbol is related to its object according to similarity—that is, by its very nature. The apophantic-representational symbol appropriates the object to itself by reproducing it in a succinct and transparent configuration. The perceptible or imaginary image of the object absorbs the symbol, or rejects it when it falls short of adequation. This absorption enhances the meaning's transparency to the point where the meaning vanishes from sight.

Appendixes

The Symbolism of Sounds

Perceptible Sign and Significiant *(Signifier).*   The perceptible sign, or sign spoken of in this study is, as we have said, the phonic or graphic configuration of the sentence produced in a communicative act (whether viewed *hic et nunc* or *in specie*). This is not, therefore, Saussure's "significiant," which is not a unit of actual communication, but a purely virtual unit, since "significiant" is a concept created for the description of the system of language (*langue*) (in the same way that "signifié" [signified] corresponds to no unit of actual signification—since this is always *of* whole sentences—although the meaning of sentences always *contains* these "signifieds," these virtual units, just as it presupposes the system of the language). The actual sentence concretizes the virtual units of language as actual ideal units, which are a part of the sentence's actual ideal unit of meaning and phonic structure. The signifier is the perceptible sign of the language (*langue*); the discourse or sentence, as a phonic configuration, is the perceptible sign of speech (*parole*).

Motivation of the Perceptible Sign of Speech.   We will now briefly refer to the old problem of the so-called motivation of the linguistic sign—a theme addressed by Dámaso Alonso in his discussion of the "poetic sign" in *Poesía Española*. In the interest of greater clarity, we must compare the terminology used in the present study with Saussure's.

Within the limits of certain conditions, a language convention can be purely arbitrary; for example, suppose a new chemical product is named "Ta." By "purely arbitrary" I mean that there is no motivation based on the nature of that product and the nature of that signifier to dictate the choice of precisely this configuration of sound and no other from among those the system makes available and eligible. The constitution of the link between "Ta" and the object named (or concept signified)—that is, the constitution of the sign (in Saussure's terminology, the unity of "signifiant" and "signifié") is arbitrary. The convention is, in this case, arbitrary. But every use of this sign (a unity, then, conventionally constituted, of a perceptible sign of the language and a meaning-concept), as the employment of a convention, is not at all arbitrary but, precisely, conventional. The link established by speaker and listener between the perceptible sign "Ta" and the object meant (or its concept), is a *motivated* linking, that is, motivated by the convention of the sign (in general, by the system of the pertinent language). The sign of a language is arbitrary, an arbitrary convention, which is not motivated by the particular nature of the sign's components; the sign of speech (*parole*) is a *motivated* use, according to convention, of the signs of a language.

The "problem of the motivation of the linguistic sign" is fraught with ambiguity; it continues to cause considerable confusion. An adequate statement of it would require that we distinguish, as we have seen, between the linguistic sign of a language (*langue*) and the linguistic sign of speech (*parole*). Except for explicit references to the sign of a language, in these analyses we always refer to the sign of speech (as in general throughout this whole book). Of course, some of our observations apply equally to the sign of a language.

Perceptible Sign of Speech as Symbol. One could properly (with systematic motivation—that is, according to convention) call the perceptible sign of speech a "symbol" if the link between the perceptible sign of speech and its meaning were viewed not as *just* conventional (based only on the corresponding system of language, inasmuch as it is an arbitrary convention), but as "naturally" based—that is, based on natural qualities of the selfsame traits of the corresponding sound configuration.[2] And this is to say: based on *similarities*. Yet what kind of similarity can exist between configurations of articulated sound and the possible objects meant—in all their limitless variety?

Of course, the acoustic sign may resemble, or imitate, the

sounds it occasionally signifies. This is the case with onomatopoeia. But acoustic phenomena constitute only one part of the universe of possible meanings. Now then, a much vaster possibility of imitation through sound occurs in the so-called "symbolism of sounds." Onomatopoetic imitation belongs with the elemental and immediate, iconic variety of imitation: the reproduction of the structure, of the intrinsic properties of the imitated object. A different type of imitation is the reproduction of the effects of the object, without reproducing its configuration or its intrinsic attributes. Objects that produce the same effect are, in this sense, *similar*. We can also add here that, just as in the case of configurational imitation, if the two objects having the same effect are associatively linked, this association or linkage is naturally based, and not simply conventionally motivated.

It is well known that certain acoustical configurations have impressive effects that are equal to the impressive effects of phenomena from the realms of the other senses. This equality of "character" or of "expression" motivates natural associations between phenomena that are themselves radically dissimilar. The spontaneous linking of phenomena of different sensory realms is known as the mental phenomenon of synesthesia. Ordinary language, in numerous common and spontaneous expressions, such as "clear voice," "brittle words," "dark vowels," "sweet tone," and "deep-toned voice," gives ample proof of the existence of synesthesia wherein one of the associated terms is a linguistic sound. The sounds of speech, then, also have an expressiveness of their own, just as other sounds do.

But this similarity of expressiveness or character is not limited to the uniting of sensations from different sensory realms, as in the case of synesthesia. We speak also of "joyful" or "frantic" or "funereal" rhythms, of "heroic" tones, etc., and these expressive attributes, which can and often are predicated on the sound configurations of discourse, can and often are, also (and originally), predicated on events, stories, attitudes, people, etc., and may thus serve to establish relations of similarity between the configurations of the sounds of discourse and the stories, people, events, etc. to which the discourse refers.[3]

That at least some linguistic sounds produce impressive effects, or have character, "expressiveness," is what makes possible, then, an occasional imitative function on their part—neither configurational nor iconic—in which the associative potential of this "expressiveness" is put to work. If the character of a particular sound configuration of discourse coincides with the character of its meaning, it can be said that the perceptible sign imitates its meaning (reproduces its impressive effect), is similar to it, and *is naturally, in addition to conventionally, linked to it.* (However, the conventional link is fundamental here, since it is the basis for all other linking in this sphere.) Thus, with respect to this phenomenon, it is proper to speak of a symbolism of sounds.

Since this coincidence of the expressiveness of the perceptible sign and the expressiveness of the meaning intensifies both and, even more, makes them patent, it is only natural that a symbolism of this type should be a fundamental possibility of lyric poetry. (See the description of its nature in Chapter III, Section 14.)

It can be averred, then, in this sense, that in cases like lyric discourse, the perceptible sign, in addition to being a conventional sign, is also a symbol.

IV. *Roman Jakobson's Conception of the Poetic Function of Language*

Two fairly recent Structuralist anthologies (*The Structuralists from Marx to Lévi-Strauss,* ed. Richard and Fernande De George, New York, Doubleday, 1972; *Strukturalismus in der Literaturwissenschaft,* ed. Heinz Blumensath, Cologne, Kiepenheuer und Witsch, 1972) reprint the article "Linguistics and Poetics" by

Roman Jakobson, originally published in the collected proceedings entitled *Style in Language* (ed. Thomas A. Sebeok, Cambridge, Mass., M.I.T. Press, 1960). Part of this article is the
eminent linguist's reflections on the functions of language and the
nature of poetic language (anticipated to a degree in the 1929
theses he developed with Jan Mukarovsky as a member of the
Prague Circle). Jakobson's concepts differ from those I set forth
in Chapters II and III above, and are akin to views that I have
criticized there as erroneous. In what follows I offer a general
critique of his influential conception, contrasting it with the modified version of Karl Bühler's model which I presented in Chapter
II.

Jakobson's first step—which supposes what is now common
dogma on the nature of poetic language—leads reflection in the
wrong direction: "Poetics deals primarily with the question,
What makes a verbal message a work of art?" If we begin with
the assumption that poetry is a verbal message, and that its nature
must be defined on this basis by a *differentia specifica*—that is,
assuming its fundamental generic identity with the different kinds
of verbal messages—we will never appropriately conceive of the
essence of the literary phenomenon. In Chapter III, above, I
explain in detail what can be summarized here as follows: if we
view poetry as a message, as real communication, it is not a
verbal event (but rather the physical presentation of the icon of an
imaginary verbal event). If we view poetry as a verbal event, it is
not primarily a *message* but an imaginary object offered to contemplation, one that only secondarily develops a nonlinguistic,
symbolic dimension—a "message"—vis-à-vis the real world.
(Would we ever say of someone who produced the precise quotation of a nonexistent linguistic act that he was delivering a verbal
message? I believe we can sense the logical dissonance in such
a description.)

In a short passage of the essay under discussion, Jakobson
hints at the radically singular nature of poetic discourse, conclud-
ing that "virtually any poetic message is a quasi-quoted discourse

with all those peculiar, intricate problems which 'speech within speech' offers to the linguist.'' But instead of conceiving of poetry as the transposition of the linguistic act and all its functions onto an imaginary plane, Jakobson, as I said, attempts to discover a specifically poetic function in the *real* linguistic act. In pursuit of this end he offers a model of linguistic communication that adds new dimensions to Bühler's model—dimensions that the author of *Sprachtheorie* apparently overlooked.

The termini of the communicative relationship that Jakobson adds to the model that we examined in Chapter II are (1) ''contact''—the physical-mental connection or channel, which establishes the relation between emitter and receiver and carries the message (I suppose that basic examples of ''channels'' would be vocal sound waves and auditory perception); (2) ''code''—the sign-system employed in communication, the language used. To the linguistic functions described by Bühler (expressive, representative, and appellative; Jakobson: ''emotive,'' ''referential,'' and ''conative''), which correspond to the situational termini of emitter, object, and receiver (Jakobson: ''addresser,'' ''context,'' and ''addressee''), Jakobson adds three more: the *metalinguistic* function (determined by the relation of message to code), the *phatic* function (determined by the conditions and characteristics of the channel [contact] itself), and the *poetic* function, determined by attention being focused on the message itself—attention that would, in a way, tend to disconnect the message from the other termini of the communicative situation and to emphasize the relations of the linguistic sign of speech with itself, that is, the internal relations of its constituent parts. ''The set (*Einstellung*) toward the *message* as such, focus on the message for its own sake, is the *poetic* function of language.''

Since Jakobson's model is in part analogous to Bühler's, we could apply to this new schema of speech the critical observations made regarding the former one. But here I will merely indicate several additional problems. First of all, this model suffers from a fundamental ambiguity: Precisely what is the message in this constellation? It is certainly not the concrete material fact of the sign, since here "channel" denotes this physical reality. Nor can the abstract perceptible sign (the "form" of the articulated sound), carried by the channel according to the principles of abstractive relevancy determined in the code, be thought of as the whole message, since "message," in the usual sense and in the technical sense in which Jakobson (as we can infer from his text) uses it, is also *what is communicated* by the perceptible sign. We already know from our Chapter II that not only the internal or ideal dimensions of discourse (the "form" of the content) are what is communicated, but also the concrete states of affairs (real or imaginary) signified by their agency. Rather, "message" is an appropriate term for the whole linguistic communication, especially if we take this primarily in its representative-referential aspect. (Rigorously stated, "message" is what we called *the communicated situation* in our Chapter II, Section 10.) It is not an adequate name for *one* constituent aspect of communication—not the appropriate terminus of an analytic view of language. Instead, "message"—like "word," "sentence," and "language"—is expressive of a synthetic view; and, for this reason, here it serves only to confuse the analytic effort represented by a model of the functions of language.

This is why, although in restricting the "poetic function" to the area of the "message" Jakobson *seems* to be delimiting and defining the field of what poetry is, in fact he does not do so, since the ambiguous denotation of the term "message" allows for its application to the communication as a whole. In practice, Jakobson's analyses of individual poems deal not only with the perceptible sign of discourse, but also with its representative, expressive, and appellative dimensions. The "message as such" becomes, then, simply the linguistic communication, and the "poetic function" of language nothing other than the absolutization of linguistic communication—that is, the *contemplation* of imaginary language, as I show in Chapter III, above. But let us examine Jakobson's theory in greater detail.

The so-called "metalinguistic function" is only one of many

species of the representative or referential function, and not, as Jakobson would have it, a new meaning-function, different from the referential one. Although the linguist (and the logician) may have a special interest in sentences in which the code used is itself spoken about (one of Jakobson's examples is "A *sophomore* is [or means] a *second-year student*"), this should not hide the fact that the code is only one among many possible objects of linguistic *reference*. In the same way that a speaker's explicit reference to himself is still reference—that is, an instance of the representative function of discourse, not to be confused with the expressive function—[1]so the description of the code itself never ceases to be description, a speaking about certain things, in which the indicative-representational dimension is dominant. There is no reason to suppose that language functions in an essentially different way when I say "a *sophomore* means a *second year student*" than when I say "two equals the square root of four," or "the blessed are immortal." And there is also no difference in the dominant meaning-function if I say "this is unlined paper," and so forth.

Examples of the "phatic"[2] function would be sentences like "Hello, do you hear me?," "Are you listening?," and exchanges like Dorothy Parker's: " 'Well!' the young man said. 'Well!' she said. 'Well, here we are!' he said. 'Here we are' she said, 'aren't we?' " Discourse such as this, Jakobson holds, serves the predominant function of assuring and prolonging verbal contact—a function that is supposedly different from the three in my model, and equally fundamental.

Undoubtedly one could speak, in reference to the kinds of discourse just exemplified, of a "contact function." But the appropriate question, as I indicated in Chapter II, is: have we to do here with a function of discourse in the same sense of "function" in which expression, representation, and appellation are functions of discourse? Phrases such as "Are you listening?" do not present a fundamental function not already included in Bühler's model. They are *questions,* a class of discourse with a special appellative dimension—because the intended effect is a particular verbal conduct on the listener's part, namely an *answer*—and a special representative dimension, namely a representation of a state of affairs as problematical. It is an interesting fact, in cases like the example-phrase, that the representative dimension of the question focuses on the very act of communication created by the sentence. But this does not constitute a basic function of dis÷ course that is different from those of the triadic model.

The second of these types of discourse, exemplified here by Dorothy Parker's dialogue, offers a quite different phenomenon, not to be confused with the previous one, although it can be said in both cases that the particular speeches have to do with the process of verbal *contact*. That is, in Dorothy Parker's exchange there is no evidence of either difficulty or effort in the adequate reception of the linguistic "message." There is nothing the least problematic about the *linguistic* contact in this case. Instead we have an example of the extralinguistic use of an apparent linguistic communication—something belonging in a class with my "pseudo-sentences" and the "performatives" of J. L. Austin. The sense, the vital function of these sentences is to create a primary, alinguistic communion of souls, which could also be accomplished through ritual acts, dance, and other forms of interhuman relations. This is the use of language referred to by Malinowski by the term "phatic communion," one instance of the kind of customary degradation of discourse that seeks to subordinate verbal action to nonlinguistic functions. Therefore, the notion of a fundamental function of language is equally inappropriate here.

In examining the model of the semantic dimensions, I stressed the necessary character of the three dimensions found—that is, I emphasized that there could be no real act of linguistic communication where even one dimension was lacking. The three dimensions *define* the act of linguistic communication (if this analytic formula be preferred to the phenomenological idiom of the description of essences). But would the "metalinguistic" and "phatic'' functions, discovered by Jakobson, be a *necessary* part of every act of linguistic communication, even if they were not always *dominant* functions?

If by "metalinguistic" we mean discourse that refers to the pertinent code, discourse in which the language used is itself spoken about, obviously not all discourse is metalinguistic. Undoubtedly the code is present and operative in all discourse, but is this presence of the code a *function* of discourse? And, even if it were, would it be a function in the same sense of the word, according to which expression, representation, and appellation are said to be functions of discourse?

Regarding the phatic function, it is clear that not all discourse has the semilinguistic character of the dialogue quoted above. On the other hand, real speech always implies, without doubt, the establishment of a psychophysical contact with the listener (even when the latter is the self-same speaker); however, if we extend the concept of the phatic function so that it covers the establishment of a psychophysical verbal contact between speakers, the term simply becomes a new and unnecessary name for the whole linguistic communication—and then, obviously, the phatic function cannot be considered one function of language among others. It therefore does not seem appropriate to the phenomenon in question to place these "functions" of Jakobson's on a level with the three fundamental ones.

Can we add anything to what we have said above about the supposed poetic function of discourse, in which the emphasis in the communication would fall on the message itself and therefore neither on the message's referent nor on its producer or receiver? Can this be called a function of language in any manageable sense of the word "function"? Would it not be more apposite to say—as I have indicated—that what we have there is a discourse or message detached from any real context, and offered thus to unrestricted contemplation—in a word, an *imaginary* discourse?

By reading the admirable pages that Jakobson has dedicated to the analysis of poems, it is easier to see what he has in mind when he speaks of this "set" (on the reader's or listener's part?) toward the message that literally constitutes the "poetic function of language." It seems fair to say that, in Jakobson's view—shared by many Structuralist critics—a text acquires a specific potentiality (precisely the "poetic function") when the relations among its different parts and elements are submitted, in addition to the general phonological, morphological, and syntactical norms of language, to ultralinguistic principles of ordering—that is, to principles not essential to an adequate and normal constitution of the meaning of the ordinary message (which, by the way, would be the same as admitting, implicitly, that the poetic function is not a fundamental function of language and should not be placed on the same level with the functions of our triad). Jakobson formulates this principle in linguistic terms when he says, "The poetic function projects the principle of equivalence from the axis of selection into the axis of combination." Obviously, this is not to be understood as saying that, in poetic discourse, the axes of selection and combination (the paradigmatic-syntagmatic system of discourse) are annulled or reversed. If such were the case, the text would be unintelligible. (Strictly speaking, such discourse is not even *imaginable*). This is why I hold that the poetic principle envisioned here is an ultralinguistic (not an extralinguistic) ordering—that is, an *additional* ordering of the forms of language, added to the primary organization of meaning that is proper to all discourse. For, clearly, Jakobson cannot mean that in poetry the syntactic links of the words disappear, as well as their usual phonological and morphological attributes.

What can be said, according to the theory under examination, and in a deliberate simplification, is that poetic discourse manifests (with undertermined frequency, I say; always, Jakobson would have to say) different systems of *repetition* of forms throughout its sequence of phonemes, syllables, words, and phrases. Rhyme, metrical rhythms, parallelisms, and the reiteration of the same objectual reference by means of different words or images, etc., are repetitive systems that project an abstract reiterative pattern upon the series of the ever-differing elements of the sequence of words. The totality of these patterns of reiteration constitutes an essential part of the "structure" of a text, in the sense this word has acquired in its use by authors such as Jakobson, Lévi-Strauss, Greimas, Riffaterre, etc. Faced with some structuralist studies, one is tempted to advance the formula that for them the relevant structure of a poetic (or mythic) text is not the discursive sequence at all, not the forward movement of an informative series built up, step by step, of additional, ever-differing elements, but instead an entity of static character, signified once and again with variations, and so enriched by the irrelevantly successive parts of the text.

In any case, in the structuralist analysis, a poetic text appears like a texture more tightly knit, and richer in internal formal relations, than ordinary discourse. The extent to which it is possible to reveal this structural weave, and just how complex this can be, is quickly surmised from the studies by Jakobson and Lévi-Strauss (in *L'Homme*, 1962) and Michael Riffaterre (in *Yale French Studies*, 1966) of the fourteen verses of Baudelaire's *Les Chats*.[3]

For our present subject, the important point to stress is our failure to find anything resembling a poetic function of language—inasmuch as it cannot be held that in *all* discourse the principle of equivalence is projected into the axis of combination, that in *all* verbal messages the linguistic elements are interwoven with functional structures that are in addition to the grammatical ones.

But even if we were to allow that there exists universally in speech something like the need for, and the function of, giving internal cohesion to the elements that make up each discourse—that is, allow that pauses, intonation, the phonic continuity itself all serve to reinforce the *unity* of a message first constructed on the lexical and grammatical level—would this be a dimension of the language that when magnified would constitute the essential moment of the phenomenon of poetry, and not simply one of the conditions of its possibility?

In any case, this aspect of the linguistic sign of speech—the cohesion of its parts—is not a dimension of the *signified* of discourse, as the functions of the triad are, and it cannot be placed on the same level with them. The structure of the sign, of the "message," is not one of its semantic functions but an enabling condition of all its semantic functions, an intrinsic descriptive characteristic of its being—not of its function of aiming at another being, that is, of its signifying. The variety and complexity of the characteristics of the act of linguistic communication are immense. I have emphasized that more than once in this book. But it has been possible to establish clear distinctions that must not be abandoned in favor of a mere accumulation of "functions of language," functions that do not constitute a genuine class of semiotic dimensions.

I will say, in passing, that I deem the supernumerary increment of the internal "fastenings" of discourse to be an enabling condition for the possibility of at least some kinds of poetry—since the structural weave constitutes an enhancement of the unity of the verbal act—but at the same time I must also say that it is a possibility created by the imaginary being of poetic discourse. Only discourse that no one truly says in our real world can be constructed as an object with autonomous architecture.

In the Structuralists' view the poetic principle of repetition or equivalency[4] is not only operative horizontally, throughout the length of the sequential series of successive elements of discourse—already mentioned above—but *vertically* as well, and at the same time, through the superposition in each textual moment of parallel messages that, while materially different, are equivalent in meaning. Thus the symbolic power of the sound-profile of discourse,[5] which in poetry usually establishes correspondences between the sounds of speech and the objects signified by it, would constitute a message *sui generis* that was the equivalent of, and parallel to, the message of the conceptual meaning of the words, as well as the message generated by the unfolding of the imagery (or the objects) projected by it.[6] The "poetic message," then, would say *the same,* not only again and again but in several ways at once! The strata of the poetic work (which Ingarden described as a polyphonic whole) would be interrelated, as are the different versions of a myth in the structural anthropology of Lévi-Strauss (see his footnote to the above-mentioned essay that he co-authored with Roman Jakobson). In a poem there would be a succession, not purely linear and forward, but at once both progressive and reiterative. As we said earlier, it is as though we were being fed different pieces of information, one after another, and by the same process on another level, one and the same information were being repeated over and over again. Just what this reiterated information is would have to be examined in each poem. But we can conjecture that in general it would have to be an *inexplicit* message, a secondary symbolic projection, whether it belonged to the expressive, the appellative, or to the representative order. For what the text of the poem clearly *says* is only occasionally a repetition, being first and foremost a sequence of different pieces of information. A poem, then, can only indirectly and in a nonimmediate and half-hidden way continually reiterate an inexplicit message. (In view of these observations, it is not surprising that there should be an affinity between structuralist descriptions and the interpretations of so-called "depth psychology.")

Of course, my present description of the structuralist theory of the poem is unilateral and extremely simplified (I have not mentioned the complexities that, in addition to the principle of equivalency, Jakobson introduces with the complementary notion of contiguity), for in this context I wanted to keep within the limits of his fundamental axiom. My purpose here is not to summarize the Structuralist theory of the poem, but to offer a critique of Jakobson's theory of the functions of language and his conception of poetry as a special function of discourse.

The valid perspectives that Jakobson opens on the theory of

poetry cannot be understood, it seems to me, as a function of real discourse that would consist in the quasi-absolutization of the message, and the neglect of its semantic dimensions—unless by "message" we are to understand the unity of all three semantic dimensions, in which case Jakobson's model would dissolve, as I indicated above, at the beginning of this Appendix. Accordingly, it is more appropriate to see in the poem an enhancement of the power of the message through an unlimited display of its three internal semantic dimensions. And since this presupposes the detaching of the message from real concrete circumstances (as we saw in Chapter III), the poetic function of discourse, I insist, is nothing other than the production of imaginary discourse.

To make this basic point clearer, I will repeat the essential steps of my reasoning in a slightly different way: The listener's or the reader's set "toward the message as such"—disregarding its reference to objects and its relations with the speaker and listener—can be taken in two ways: as primary attention to the *signifier* (in its phonetic, prosodic, or morphological properties), or, in its totality, to the linguistic *sign* of the speech as the unity of signifiers and signifieds. The second way of understanding this definitory formula of poetry is the one that Jakobson adheres to in his own analyses of poetry, which are not limited to an analysis of word-sounds and their structures. But this interpretation of his formula implies a recognition of the internal semantic dimensions of discourse—that is, of the ideal and imaginary projection of the object referred to, of the speaker, and of the listener. If the represented object, the speaker, and the listener, as imaginary presences, form a part of the "message," then the *Einstellung* or "set" toward the message as such is the disposition of the receiver toward that kind of absolutization of the discourse which places it beyond all real concrete situations, and releases the internal dimensions of signification at the imaginary level. That is, the poetic function of discourse is not a function of discourse on a par with the other functions, but the phenomenon of a whole discourse that is ontically different from real discourse.

V. *Barbara Herrnstein Smith's and Richard Ohmann's Views of the Language of Literature*

The Notion of a Fictive Entity

In several publications since 1970 and especially in *On the Margins of Discourse: The Relation of Literature to Language* (University of Chicago Press, 1978), Barbara Herrnstein Smith has expressed the same insight into the nature of literature which gives rise to one of the basic theses of my book: that literary discourse is fictive discourse, not words the author is *saying*. Without any knowledge of my publications, of course, she comes in places to strikingly similar formulations and emphases. It seems to me, however, that my inquiry went a step further along that path, and that her concept of fictive discourse lacks essential distinctions that are drawn in my text. The following remarks will explain this.

There is a widely shared reluctance to discuss fiction, and art in general, in terms of the opposition of "fictitious" and "real," or of merely imaginary events and actual fact. This reluctance and its motives could be exemplified by certain passages in Nelson Goodman's *Languages of Art: An Approach to a Theory of Symbols* (Indianapolis, 1968), especially the chapter entitled "Fictions"—to mention a work Barbara Smith approvingly points to in her book, although with reference to other, related matters. The main reason for avoiding that conceptual framework concerns the well known paradoxes involved in the notion of a nonreal or nonexistent object. This might explain—here I am, of course, guessing—why Professor Smith chose to discuss fictive discourse not under the defining opposition of "fictitious" and "real" but under the opposition (in my opinion inappropriate here) of "fictive" and "natural." In doing so, she first assimilates "fictive" to "designed," "artificial," "playful," "mimetic" (whereby she comes close to Richard Ohmann's and John Searle's concept of fictional discourse as "pretended," "nonserious" speech).[1] This is the notion of fiction as what is *feigned*, inauthentic, adulterated, and in this sense not natural.

As I see it, a second set of Professor Smith's determinations defines "natural" discourse as an historical event, something that has happened at a definite time and place, a verbal action that is a part of (spatiotemporal) nature, while fictive events are declared to be historically (that is, spatiotemporally) indeterminate. I cannot see this as anything but a circumlocution for the opposition of real and fictitious, since one of the classic definitions of real being (explicitly used, for example, by Roman Ingarden) is precisely spatiotemporal occurrence. Third, and finally, fictive discourse is defined as a *representation* of discourse, but also as *represented* discourse. This ambiguity occurs several times and pervades a good part of her discussion.

I think that these determinations are inexact and unnecessarily inconsistent. If direct, serious speech (certainly a "cultural" fact) is a part of nature, why should playful speaking not be a part of it? What notion of nature allows this severance? Certainly not purposelessness. And certainly not a lack of institutional or conventional presuppositions and rules. Why, indeed, should not imitations and representations (verbal or not) be said to be a part of nature, if discourses in theology or numismatics are said to be a part of it? Obviously, the concept of the artificial versus the natural does not apply to the distinction of fictive and nonfictive discourse.

According to Professor Smith, fictive discourses are representations, as *Hamlet* is "a representation, not an instance, of a man avenging his father's murder" (p. 8). But if fictive discourses are representations, I cannot see why they would not be "historical events." There certainly has never been a representation of *Hamlet* or a reading of it or a thought about it or image of it that did not occur at a definite place and time in our historical world (except, precisely, representations that are only the subject of fictional narration). Moreover, while Shakespeare's Prince Hamlet (as well as any fictive individual, be it person, event, object, or discourse) has to be thought of as a singular, individual entity, it is clear that the representations of this unique individual constitute a *class* of more or less similar events (theatrical performances, private readings, and so forth). There is an ontic abyss between the representation of a fictive person or of a fictive speech and the represented fictive person or fictive speech. Although any representation (that is not itself a represented fictitious one) belongs to a class of historical (real) events, the represented fictive entities are individuals that never had temporal and spatial actuality in our real historical world. In some passages, Professor Smith comes close to formulating this view, one clearly inconsistent with her concept of fictive discourse as representation· The text of a poem, she says, is like the score of a musical composition or the script of a play; it "tells us, in other words, how to produce the verbal act it represents" (p. 31). Fictive discourse, then, appears here as *represented* discourse. Nevertheless, it is an essential point of this whole matter, as I understand it, that we can never produce the fictive discourse, we can only produce and reproduce its representation. Indeed, we produce and reproduce the representation of fictitious discourse in different media: in the textual inscription, the vocal performance, the mental pseudo-vocalization of silent reading, or simply the mental image of heard or written discourse: these are all instances and kinds of pseudo-sentences—that is, of iconic representations of discourse. The question, now, of how we can experience the fictitious if we can only produce and reproduce its representation brings us to the paradoxes about fiction that I mentioned at the beginning of this chapter. But these paradoxes are not to be sidestepped; they must be confronted, because they reveal the nature of the phenomenon of fiction, and because, as we see, they reappear no matter how resolutely we try to avoid them. I cannot develop their analysis here, but I must indicate in reference to these paradoxes that the motives leading to the ambiguities I am criticizing are powerful; they derive from the nature of representation. I think that this ambiguity of the thing itself is what Professor Smith has in mind when she alludes to "the duplicity of art" in a short passage at the end of her chapter 2 (pp. 39–40).

She states that "a poem is never spoken, not even by the poet himself. It is always re-cited" (p. 31), that "the events represented in the play are historically indeterminate" (p. 34), and that "the poem refers to and denotes nothing" (p. 10). These are half-truths, the last an often-asserted inexactitude. They are true statements in only one of the two pertinent respects, namely in the context of reality proper—that is, in the real context of the representation, not in the purely imaginary context of the represented fictitious discourse. The adequate reception of a poem includes its understanding as the original (fictive) discourse of a unique (fictive) speaker, and also as a definite reference to certain determinate things. Can we read the Shakespearean line of one of Professor Smith's examples, "To me, fair friend, you never can be old . . . ," without sensing in imagination a singular verbal event and understanding a reference to a person known to the speaker? Otherwise, how could we create the context of the fictive utterance, a creation that, according to Professor Smith, constitutes the basic interpretation of the poem by the reader? That the speaker, the speech, the reference it makes, and the things referred to are all fictive—that is, properly nonexistent—does not make them less a speaker, a speech, a reference, and things referred to, as Kant indicated for imagined entities in general in his discussion of the ontological proof of the existence of God.[2]

That fictive utterances are "*possible* utterances, but not actual ones" (p. 52) does not go well with their supposedly being representations or performances, nor (and this is more important) with their phenomenal character: we do not listen to poems as to *possible* sentences (or as to *hypothetical* sentences, as some other theoreticians say), unless they are (and this should be rare) fictive discourses that have the form of hypotheses or of contemplated possible utterances (something like: "Shall I tell her: '*be my love*'?" or "I look at the stars and I think: *perhaps the universe is but a glass wheel*"). Fictive utterances are basically fictive *actual* sayings of fictive speakers.

The contradictions we have criticized can be avoided if we distinguish the representation of discourse (real verbal configurations that are nonetheless pseudo-sentences, not said but made to evoke sentences that are said) and the represented discourse (authentic sayings of someone that are either real past events or fictitious events merely imagined). Poetic or (*sensu stricto*) literary discourse is not defined by being a *representation* of discourse (since any transcript of historical discourse is also that), or by being *represented* discourse (since the historical discourse transcribed is also represented discourse), but by being a merely imaginary discourse represented by a conventionally designed pseudo-verbal icon.

What I have said could be misleading for those of my readers who have not yet read Smith's book if I did not now add that there she has developed many points far beyond anything I have said in mine. Especially important for a theory of literature, it seems to me, are her analyses of the determination of meaning by the nature of speech as *event* (chapter 2), and her illuminating study of how a fictive "message" can become "natural"—that is, a real message (chapter 3).

Feigned Speech: A Useless Notion

Richard Ohmann, too, comes close to the comprehension of literature as purely imaginary discourse, and the reader will find several passages in his articles that resemble certain of mine.[3]

Nonetheless, our conceptions diverge. Poems are "quasi-speech-acts," according to Professor Ohmann (*Philosophy and Rhetoric*, Vol. 4, p. 12). One is reminded of Ingarden's definition of literary sentences as "quasi-statements." A literary work, Ohmann continues, presents discourses detached from the necessary circumstances of speech, and literary discourse, therefore, "is a discourse without illocutionary force." But then, considering that the reader constructs or imagines the appropriate circumstances of the discourse, he admits a "mimetic" illocutionary force attached to the imaginary "quasi-speech-acts."

Why then, I would ask, are they said to be *quasi*-speech-acts, and not entirely and thoroughly speech acts, since they are acknowledged to be as imaginary as their circumstances and their illocutionary force? Are these "quasi-circumstances" and "quasi-forces"? Is the literary speech itself (the *locutionary* act) also merely a quasi-speech? I am not suggesting that such a theory would be a logical impossibility (provided some minor formal adjustments were made). What I maintain is that there is nothing in our common experience of literature to support the idea (also found in J. L. Austin's notion of "parasitic" speech) that language and action in poetry or fiction are *intrinsically* less language and less action than in ordinary experience. The deprivation affecting literary language is a radical one, but it is not in the field of describable attributes, it is the lack of the attribute of proper existence—that is, the fact of its being purely imaginary.[4]

Because he does not arrive, in my view, at a clear distinction of the acts of the real author and the acts of the fictional speakers (a distinction I have grounded in the concepts of iconically representing and real pseudo-sentences, on the one hand, and represented fictitious sentences, on the other), avoidable ambiguities persist in Ohmann's analyses. For example, he defines the work of the writer of literature as an act of "pretending" to quote or report the discourse of another (imaginary) person. I assume writers and readers know that the game of literature is one of imagination and that the writer does not merely pretend to provide the signs for the production or reproduction of the imaginary experience he has invented (using the institutional framework of literary tradition), but actually *does* provide them. After all, if the writer were only pretending that, he would not be really doing it, and then the point of Ohmann's argument (that literary discourse is reported imaginary speech) would vanish.[5]

Needless to say I have considered Richard Ohmann's analyses only in relation to the ones I present in this book. Most of his contributions do not pertain to my circumscribed subject.[6]

Notes

Preface

1. For the history and nature of phenomenological criticism, see Robert R. Magliola, *Phenomenology and Literature* (West Lafayette, Ind., Purdue University Press, 1977).

Chapter I. *The Logical Nature and Phenomenal Structure of Literary Narrative*

1. Josef König's lectures of 1953 and 1954 on "Theoretical and Practical Sentences" dealt, among other things, with such distinctions. The text of the lectures is being prepared for publication by Günther Patzig and Fritz Gebhardt, under the auspices of the Deutsche Forschungsgemeinschaft.

2. This is the basic, traditional structure of narrative. On the modifications that have taken place in modern literature, see my article "Die logische Struktur der Dichtung," in *Deutsche Vierteljahrsschrift für Literaturwissenschaft und Geistesgeschichte,* Vol. XLVII, No. 2 (Stuttgart, Metzler, 1973), pp. 185–200, as well as Section 17 of this book. It should be remarked here that the notion of "logic of narratives" has been used (by Claude Bremond—*Logique du récit,* Paris, Seuil, 1973—and other French critics) in a sense different from the traditional one that determines my own analysis. The field of Bremond's "logic" is akin to that of the so-called "narrative grammars," and is, in fact, a theory of the structure of actions.

Notes

3. The possibility of dramatic irony lies in an analogous logical structure. Of course, "reality," in the theater, is established not by a narrator's statements but by the (imaginary) occurrences of the play, which in turn are determined by the real stage performances (pseudo-actions that structurally correspond to what we will define as the pseudo-sentences of the literary text—Section 13). If a narrative is told not by one basic narrator but by several narrators belonging to the same imaginary level, obviously the logical structure is not the traditional and elementary one we are describing. The quality of "reality" or "truth" of the story can thereby be substantially modified. See above, note 2.

4. We touch here on a matter that has been a major theme of phenomenological research since Edmund Husserl's description of the "Neutralitätsmodifikation" in *Logische Untersuchungen* (Halle, 1900), trans. J. N. Findlay, *Logical Investigations* (New York, Humanities Press, 1970), Fifth Investigation, chapters 3–5; also in *Ideen zu einer reinen Phänomenologie und phänomenologischen Philosophie* (Halle, 1913), trans. W. R. Boyce Gibson, *Ideas: General Introduction to Pure Phenomenology* (London, Allen and Unwin, 1931), pars. 109–114, 117.

5. Josef König, *Sein und Denken* (Halle, Niemeyer, 1934; Tübingen, Niemeyer, 1969).

6. A discussion of unreliability in fiction and of alternative or deviant logical structures of literary narrative is presented below in Section 17.

7. *Aesthetic as Science of Expression and General Linguistic,* trans. Douglas Ainslie (London, Macmillan, 1909; New York, Noonday Press, 1953).

8. In Chapter III we will see that it is more exact to distinguish the narrator from the perceptible signs of his sentences.

9. The technical distinction between the *represented* or *said* and the *expressed* or *manifested* is developed in Chapter II. See also below, Chapter II, note 4.

Chapter II. *The Structure of Linguistic Signification: Semantic Dimensions of Language*

1. *Sprachtheorie* (Jena, G. Fischer, 1934; Stuttgart, G. Fischer, 1965).
2. See S. J. Schmidt, *Texttheorie* (Munich, Fink, 1973).
3. "Semantische Funktionen," in *Sprachtheorie,* p. 28.
4. Throughout this book "expression" and "manifestation" are used synonymously to designate the function of speech that makes the internal states of the speaker perceptible in a way different from speaking of and about those states or linguistically representing them. This concept of "expression" is related to the notion of "emotive meaning" in C. K. Ogden and I. A. Richards, *The Meaning of Meaning* (New York, Harcourt, Brace, 1925), but has a wider

connotation. The only exceptions to this terminological use are the passages in which I comment on Husserl's theory of meaning, since this author uses "expression" (*Ausdruck*) to designate the meaningful sign. There I use only "manifestation" for the function indicated. "Manifestation," by the way, seems to be the best translation of Husserl's corresponding *Kundgabe*. Bühler uses both *Kundgabe* and *Ausdruck* in this sense. See also R. Barthes, *Elements of Semiology*, trans. Annette Lavers and Colin Smith (New York, Hill and Wang, 1968), IV.2, "Connotation."

5. Bruno Snell, *Der Aufbau der Sprache* (Hamburg, Claassen, 1952).

6. Husserl, *Logical Investigations*, I, "Expression and Meaning," chapter 1.

7. Charles Bally, *Le langage et la vie* (Geneva, Edition Atar, 1913).

8. *Logical Investigations*, I, chapter 1; *Sprachtheorie*, par. 2.

9. Josef König, *Sein und Denken*, par. 1.

10. *An Inquiry into Meaning and Truth* (London, Allen and Unwin, 1940), chapter 14.

11. Dámaso Alonso, *Poesía española* (Madrid, Gredos, 1951), "Significante y significado."

12. Friedrich Kainz, *Psychologie der Sprache* (Stuttgart, Enke, 1954), Vol. I, Part Three (III. Hauptstück).

13. "... drei weitgehend unabhängig variablen Sinnbezügen ..." (*Sprachtheorie*, p. 28).

14. See the summary of Husserl's theory of meaning, in Appendix I.

15. See below, Section 10.

16. *Psychologie der Sprache*, Vol. I, pp. 172 ff. Regarding the varieties of signs, see Barthes, *Elements of Semiology*, II.1.

17. *An Inquiry into Meaning and Truth*, chapter 14.

18. Real speech appears to be a part of praxis rather than of theory, in spite of Croce's insistence on the theoretic-aesthetic function of language (*Aesthetic*, passim).

19. Despite the community of the communicated situation for both speaker and listener, it can be said that each of them finds himself in a different personal situation within the shared one and, besides, may actually be in another one that he does not perceive.

20. Jean-Paul Sartre developed his theory of literature from similar observations: "Qu'est-ce que la littérature?" *Situations II* (Paris, Gallimard, 1948), trans. Bernard Frechtman, *What Is Literature?* (New York, Harper and Row, 1965). In Chapter III, below, I propose a radical modification of the view that literature has the structure and nature of communication.

21. Bertrand Russell touches inconclusively on these questions in his *An Inquiry into Meaning and Truth*, especially chapter 1, "What Is a Word?"

22. *This* opposition of ideal generality and concrete individual does not

correspond to the Saussurean opposition *langue/parole*. It is not the ideality of the *system* that is meant here, but the ideality of a *class* of occurrences.

23. *Logical Investigations*, I, chapter 1. See also Roman Ingarden, *Das literarische Kunstwerk* (Halle, Niemeyer, 1931; Tübingen, Niemeyer, 1965), trans. George G. Grabowicz, *The Literary Work of Art* (Evanston, Northwestern University Press, 1974), par. 25. This points to the phenomenon of "alienation" or transmutation of mimetic discourse that is described in Chapter I of the present book. For a more detailed analysis, see below, Appendix 1.

24. Real speech can be neither without its situation nor separated from it. There are linguistic signs that have lost their place, but no unplaced speeches, despite Bühler's assumption of "situationsferne Reden" (*Sprachtheorie*, p. 23).

Chapter III. *Language and Literature*

1. Charles Morris, *Signs, Language, and Behavior* (New York, Prentice-Hall, 1946). Charles Sanders Peirce, *Collected Papers*, Vol. II, *Elements of Logic* (Cambridge, Mass., Harvard University Press, 1932), Book II, chapters 2 and 3, especially chapter 2, par. 5.

2. Similarly, what is perceptually given on the theatrical stage is the iconic sign of the imaginary actions and speeches of the represented drama.

3. These pseudo-sentences or pseudo-speeches should not be confused with the common subordinate sentence, which does not have the properties indicated above. Example-sentences such as those which appear in theoretical discussions on language are pseudo-sentences and signify iconically imaginary sentences. Not all written or recorded sentences are pseudo-sentences. Graphic signs are often produced for the sake of communication, and not as representatives of actually pronounced sentences. To produce a recorded message, on the other hand, one has actually to pronounce "sentences," but this phonic utterance is not an authentic sentence, not a linguistic sign for an addressee (and it is not produced with that understanding); it is a means of producing perceptible signs with a recording—another kind, therefore, of pseudo-sentence.

4. Wolfgang Kayser, *Das sprachliche Kunstwerk* (Bern, Francke, 1948). Günther Müller, "Über die Seinsweise von Dichtung," *Deutsche Vierteljahrsschrift für Literaturwissenschaft und Geistesgeschichte*, Vol. XVII, No. 2 (1939), pp. 137–152. Alfonso Reyes, *La experiencia literaria* (Buenos Aires, Losada, 1952), p. 65. René Wellek and Austin Warren, *Theory of Literature* (New York, Harcourt Brace, 1949), chapter 12.

5. ". . . poems are as silent as statues" (Northrop Frye, *Anatomy of Criticism*, Princeton, Princeton University Press, 1957, "Polemical Introduction").

6. Wolfgang Kayser, "Wer erzählt den Roman?", in *Die Vortragsreise* (Bern, Francke, 1958), and *Entstehung und Krise des modernen Romans* (Stuttgart, Metzler, 1955). A full development of this theme has been presented by Wolfgang Iser in his *Der implizite Leser* (Munich, Fink, 1972), trans. *The Implied Reader* (Baltimore, Johns Hopkins University Press, 1974). See also Gerald Prince "Introduction a l'étude du narrataire," *Poétique*, 14 (Paris, Seuil, 1973).

7. *The Rhetoric of Fiction* (Chicago, The University of Chicago Press, 1961).

8. *Sprachtheorie*, par. 2.

9. This term has been used to designate the most general division of literature by José Ortega y Gasset, *Meditaciones del Quijote* (Madrid, Calpe, 1914), and Reyes, *La experiencia literaria*. The traditional designation "natural species of poetry" ("Naturarten der Poesie") derives from Goethe's *Noten und Abhandlungen zum West-Östlichen Diwan.*

10. This observation can be related to T. S. Eliot's concept of the poetic "objective correlative," first stated in the essay "Hamlet and His Problems," *Athenaeum*, 4665 (London, 1919), pp. 940–941, and his *The Sacred Wood*, (London, Methuen, 1920).

11. On this point one might attempt to relate these considerations to the theories of lyric poetry of Emil Staiger and Josef König: Staiger, *Grundbegriffe der Poetik* (Zürich, Atlantis, 1952); König, "Die Natur der ästhetischen Wirkung," in *Wesen und Wirklichkeit des Menschen: Festschrift für Helmuth Plessner* (Göttingen, Vandenhoeck und Ruprecht, 1957).

12. What we say, we know already; what we *express,* we can grasp only after it has been objectified through the utterance. The expressed, as we saw in Chapter II, above, is to a certain extent a product of what is said. I think Husserl is wrong to view as necessarily imaginary any communication of the subject with himself. The solitary monologue is real and has real functions. Husserl, of course, is primarily concerned with the representative function (*Logical Investigations*, I, chapter 1).

13. Not all situations of this type will be "lyrical." Not all that has been called lyric poetry will fit into this type of communicative situation. However, there is a traditional notion of lyricity that corresponds to this situational structure. See Kayser, *Das sprachliche Kunstwerk*, chapter 10; also Staiger, *Grundbegriffe der Poetik*, pp. 13 ff. A borderline case is the dramatic soliloquy; it, too, is an utterance that substantially aims at the production of a mood, although rather than a lyric mood, this one is a tempering for action. It should be noticed that the coincidence of speaker and listener in solitary speech tends to collapse the distinction between expressive and appellative meaning.

14. Kayser, *Das sprachliche Kunstwerk*, chapter 10, par. 4. Staiger,

Notes

Grundbegriffe der Poetik, pp. 85 ff. Thomas Mann, *The Magic Mountain,* trans. H. T. Lowe-Porter (New York, Knopf, 1958), prologue.

15. These genre-structures admit further specifications, and encompass types and subtypes. See Franz Stanzel, *Typische Formen des Romans* (Göttingen, Vandenhoeck und Ruprecht, 1965), and *Die typischen Erzählsituationen im Roman* (Vienna and Stuttgart, Braumüller, 1955), trans. James P. Pusack, *Narrative Situations in the Novel* (Bloomington, Ind., Indiana University Press, 1971). The complex system of the universe of literature presented by Northrop Frye in his *Anatomy of Criticism* has foundations very different from the tripartition suggested here. Paul Hernadi, in his *Beyond Genre* (Ithaca, Cornell University Press, 1972) and in subsequent articles, has been developing a system of literary forms that considers both the features of the communicative process and the nature of the contents. See also Seymour Chatman's *Story and Discourse* (Ithaca, Cornell University Press, 1978).

16. Staiger, *Grundbegriffe der Poetik,* pp. 82, 188.

17. The characters, moreover, can produce (imaginary) pseudo-sentences, and thus communicate imaginary sentences (which will be imaginary to the second degree).

18. *An Inquiry into Meaning and Truth,* chapter 14.

19. On this question see Michael Scriven and Mary Macdonald, "Language in Fiction," *Proceedings of the Aristotelian Society,* Supplementary Volume XXVIII, *Belief and Will* (London, 1954); Barbara Herrnstein Smith, *On the Margins of Discourse: The Relation of Literature to Language* (Chicago, University of Chicago Press, 1978); John Searle, "The Logical Status of Fictional Discourse," *New Literary History,* Vol. VI (Charlottesville, The University of Virginia, 1975), pp. 319–332; F. Martínez-Bonati, "Die logische Struktur der Dichtung," *Deutsche Vierteljahrsschrift für Literaturwissenschaft und Geistesgeschichte,* 1973, and "The Act of Writing Fiction," *New Literary History,* Vol. XI (1980), pp. 425–434.

20. R. Ingarden, *Vom Erkennen des literarischen Kunstwerkes* (Tübingen, Niemeyer, 1968), trans. Ruth A. Crowley and Kenneth R. Olson, *The Cognition of the Literary Work of Art* (Evanston, Ill., Northwestern University Press, 1974).

21. Roland Barthes, *S/Z,* trans. Richard Miller (New York, Hill and Wang, 1974).

22. Ingarden, *Das literarische Kunstwerk,* chapter 10.

23. "Algunos tópicos estructuralistas y la esencia de la poesía," *Revista Canadiense de Estudios Hispánicos,* Vol. II, No. 3 (1978), pp. 195–215.

24. Some theorists (for example, A. J. Greimas) call this the "verisimilitude" of the work, meaning the law that determines what is credible or

possible in the pertinent world. I prefer to avoid this expression here because verisimilitude has been, since Aristotle, a term for one kind of constitutive law of fiction—the one that conforms to the notions held by the public as to what is credible. And it has become, through the tradition of realism in modern literature, a notion limited to an imagination bound to the features of common everyday experience. To use this word in a new terminological sense is unnecessarily confusing.

25. See my "Cervantes y las regiones de la imaginación," *Dispositio,* Vol. II, No. 1 (1977), pp. 28-53.

26. Not only the term "stream of consciousness" but also the epistemological and metaphysical questions relating mind and objectivity that arise from reflections like the present ones fall within William James's domain.

Appendix I. *The Phenomenon of Alienation of the Mimetic Content of Narrative Sentences*

1. For a more detailed discussion of this subject, see my "La concepción del lenguaje en la filosofía de Husserl," *Anales de la Universidad de Chile* (Santiago, 1959-60).

2. As already mentioned, Husserl insists on the necessity of thinking of these examples as serious and effective speech.

3. Russell, *An Inquiry into Meaning and Truth,* chapter 12, points to the same phenomenon when he states: "Only true sentences succeed in indicating."

4. *Logical Investigations,* I, 15, 4.

5. Husserl devotes par. 14 of the First Investigation to the distinction of three possible meanings of the equivocal term "content of an expression": (1) content as intentional meaning, sense, signification; (2) content as fulfilling sense, and (3) content as object. The singular apophantic content of a narrative is signification before its alienation, and, then, imaginary fulfilling sense. In literary fiction, the imaginary fulfilling sense is the substantial part of the object (unless one considers fiction as discourse without object).

6. *Das literarische Kuntswerk* (1931), p. 170.

7. Croce, in his *Aesthetic,* highlights this opposition of image and concept. And Husserl, in his "First Investigation," insists on the difference between illustrative images and general concepts. Nevertheless, while Croce identifies intuition with the production of images, Husserl recognizes an intuition of essences, of generalities.

Notes

Appendix II. *A Transcendental Aesthetic and Logic of the Literary Experience*

1. The nonexistence of the particular *transcendent* object is here an immanent, intrinsic feature of the corresponding meaning-intention; the particular
object is thought of as nonexistent. The effective reality of the world, regarding
this particular object, is irrelevant for this aesthetic game of the imagination.

2. Nontranscendency is "el imperativo genérico del arte": *Ideas sobre la
novela* (Madrid, 1925), trans. Helene Weyl, *The Dehumanization of Art and
Notes on the Novel* (Princeton, Princeton University Press, 1948).

3. *Das literarische Kunstwerk,* par. 25.

4. I refer to the observations made in various parts of this book about the way
the reader projects and understands the poetic object: this is intentionally meant
as a concrete speech emerging from a singular circumstance; the narrative-
descriptive statements of the basic narrator are taken as absolutely true; at the
same time, the narrated events are understood as being fictitious; etc. Jonathan
Culler, in his *Structuralist Poetics* (Ithaca, Cornell University Press, 1975),
has called for a new poetics grounded in the analysis of literary competence and
the rules of literary reading. Wolfgang Iser's *Der Akt des Lesens* (Munich,
Fink, 1976), trans. *The Act of Reading* (Baltimore, Johns Hopkins University
Press, 1978), is a comprehensive study of this matter, as is Roman Ingarden's
The Cognition of the Literary Work of Art. I have indicated in the Preface,
above, my own publications on the subject.

5. Without contradiction it can be said that these functionally necessary
beliefs are suspended through the encompassing ironic awareness of play. Put
another way: one enters knowingly into the realm of the imaginary, but once
inside, one cannot distinguish it from the real. Coleridge's much quoted formula
for "poetic faith"—"a willing suspension of disbelief" (*Biographia Literaria,*
II, 6), points in a similar way to this radical change of intellectual attitude which
constitutes the fictional frame of mind.

6. See F. Martínez-Bonati, "Erzählungsstruktur und ontologische Schichtenlehre," in *Erzählforschung I,* ed. W. Haubrichs (Göttingen, Vandenhoeck und
Ruprecht, 1976).

7. See a different account of these phenomena in Käte Hamburger's "Das
epische Praeteritum," *Deutsche Vierteljahrsschrift für Literaturwissenschaft
und Geistesgeschichte,* Vol. XXVII, No. 3 (1953), pp. 329–357, and *Die Logik
der Dichtung* (Stuttgart, Klett, 1957), trans. Marilynn J. Rose, *The Logic of
Literature* (Bloomington, Indiana University Press, 1973).

8. *Aesthetic,* chapter 1.

Appendix III. *Toward a Concept of the Linguistic Symbol*

1. *Poesía española*, chapter "Significante y significado." Similarity as connection between the symbol and the symbolized appears in Wittgenstein's early theory of the sentence as a structural correspondence of the "picture" and the sentence to the state of affairs to which it refers (*Tractatus logico-philosophicus*, 2.12, 2.15, 3, and passim).

2. The signifier could be called a symbol if the convention that establishes the linguistic sign were not arbitrary, but were grounded in the nature of both the signifier and the signified. This is the problem of Plato's *Cratylus*.

3. Observations such as these make possible an understanding of the Aristotelian dictum that, regarding character, music "is the most imitative of the arts" (*Politics*, VIII. 5). For a systematic study of synesthetic and, more generally, "expressive" or connotative affinities between different kinds of objects, see Charles E. Osgood et al., *The Measurement of Meaning* (Urbana, Ill., University of Illinois Press, 1957, 1967), and *Cross-Cultural Universals of Affective Meaning* (Urbana, Ill., University of Illinois Press, 1975). I touch on the question of these secondary or indirect attributes of things in "Über ästhetische Urteile," *Archiv für Philosophie*, Vol. IX, Nos. 1-2 (Stuttgart, Kohlhammer, 1959), pp. 112-128, and in "Nicht-intentionale oder expressive Qualitäten," *Argumentationen, Festschrift für Josef König* (Göttingen, Vandenhoeck und Ruprecht, 1964).

Appendix IV. *Roman Jakobson's Conception of the Poetic Function of Language*

1. I have emphasized this point in Section 9, above.

2. If "phatic" is derived from "phanai" (Greek: to say, to speak), it should properly mean "of the nature of, or related to, speech." Jakobson refers to Bronislaw Malinowski's "The Problem of Meaning in Primitive Languages" (in Ogden and Richards, *The Meaning of Meaning*, Supplement I) as the source of his nonetymological use of the term. I find, however, that, in his article, Malinowski does not speak of a *phatic function* of language, but rather of a function of "phatic communion"—that is, a communion of souls through speech. This slippage of meaning has found its way into the dictionary, as in *Webster's New Collegiate Dictionary*, 1976 edition.

3. Roman Jakobson and Claude Lévi-Strauss, "'Les Chats' de Charles Baudelaire," *L'Homme*, No. 2 (Paris, Mouton, 1962), pp. 5-21, trans. in *The*

Notes

Structuralists from Marx to Lévi-Strauss, cited above. Michael Riffaterre, "Describing Poetic Structures: Two Approaches to Baudelaire's *Les Chats,*" *Yale French Studies,* No. 36-37 (New Haven, Yale University, 1966), pp. 200-242.

4. Emil Staiger underlines the preeminence of repetition as a structural principle of lyric poetry, and provides a phenomenological account of this formal fact (*Grundbegriffe der Poetik*).

5. See above, Appendix III.

6. The correspondences of signifier and signified described by Dámaso Alonso in *Poesía española* belong to this kind of vertical relation between the strata of the literary work.

Appendix V. *Barbara Herrnstein Smith's and Richard Ohmann's Views of the Language of Literature*

1. See Searle, "The Logical Status of Fictional Discourse," cited above, Chapter III, note 19. I refer to Ohmann's statements below.

2. *Critique of Pure Reason,* trans. Norman Kemp Smith (London, Macmillan, 1929), Second Division, Book II, chapter 3, section 4.

3. See especially "Speech Acts and the Definition of Literature," *Philosophy and Rhetoric,* Vol. IV, No. 1 (University Park, Pennsylvania, Pennsylvania University Press, 1971), pp. 1-19; also "Speech, Action, and Style," *Literary Style: A Symposium,* ed. Seymour Chatman (London and New York, Oxford University Press, 1971), and "Speech, Literature, and the Space Between," *New Literary History,* Vol. IV (Charlottesville, The University of Virginia, 1972-73), pp. 47-63.

4. Despite Hegel's emphatic rejection of it in his *Logic,* Kant's distinction of "real predicates," on the one hand, and the predicate of existence, on the other, has persisted and can be found, in substance, in statements like Frege's *Function und Begriff* (Jena, Pohle, 1891) and G. E. Moore's "Is Existence a Predicate?" *Proceedings of the Aristotelian Society,* Supplementary Volume XV (London, 1936).

5. Since my paper criticizing the notion of the writer's act as one of pretending has appeared in a readily accessible journal, I will not repeat its argument here.

6. Mary Louise Pratt, *Toward a Speech Act Theory of Literary Discourse* (Bloomington, Ind., Indiana University Press, 1977), also comments critically on these articles by Ohmann. My views correspond to hers only in part. In my opinion her understanding of the fictive nature of literary discourse is not radical enough. As a consequence, she overlooks the fact that the ontic difference

(fictitiousness) determines an intrinsic difference in the structure of literary speech. I am referring to the *fantastic* possibilities of fictive speech situations (see above, Section 17).

Index of Authors

(This list does not include translators or editors.)

173

Index of Authors

Index of Subjects

Index of Subjects

Library of Congress Cataloging in Publication Data

Martínez Bonati, Félix.
  Fictive discourse and the structures of literature.

  Translation of La estructura de la obra literaria.
  Includes bibliographical references and index.
  1. Literature—Philosophy. 2. Psycholinguistics.
I. Title.
PN45.M38513 1981   808'.00141   80-23628
ISBN 0-8014-1308-7